The
CHANGING
SEX
DIFFERENTIAL
in
MORTALITY

The
CHANGING
SEX
DIFFERENTIAL
in
MORTALITY

Robert D. Retherford

INTERNATIONAL POPULATION AND URBAN RESEARCH
UNIVERSITY OF CALIFORNIA, BERKELEY

Studies in Population and Urban Demography No. 1

GREENWOOD PRESS
Westport, Connecticut ● London, England

Library of Congress Cataloging in Publication Data

Retherford, Robert D
    The changing sex differential in mortality.

    (Studies in population and urban demography; no. 1)
    Bibliography: p.
    Includes index.
    1. Mortality. 2. Sex—Statistics. I. Title.
II. Series. [DNLM: 1. Mortality. 2. Sex factors.
HB1323.S5 R438c]
HB1323.S5R47   301.32'2   74-19808
ISBN 0-8371-7848-7

Library of Congress Catalog Card Number: 74-19808
ISBN: 0-8371-7848-7

First published in 1975

Greenwood Press, a division of Williamhouse-Regency Inc.
51 Riverside Avenue, Westport, Connecticut 06880

Manufactured in the United States of America

Contents

Tables

Foreword

Of all changes in the world since 1750, one of the most conse-
quential is the drastic and unprecedented fall in human mortality.
The average length of life in Western countries has more than
doubled, going from around 35 years to around 73. A similar
change has occurred more recently and more quickly in the
less developed regions. Without this spectacular improvement,
many other major transformations would not have occurred.
The high level of urbanization and the explosive growth of world
population, for example, would both have been impossible.
Indeed, it is hard to imagine modern society without the low
mortality that influences every aspect of it.

In view of its importance in modern history, our research
office has sponsored several investigations of mortality changes
and their effects. Two of these were by Dr. Eduardo E. Arriaga—
*New Life Tables for Latin American Populations in the Nine-
teenth and Twentieth Centuries* (1968) and *Mortality Decline
and Its Demographic Effects in Latin America* (1970); and one
was by Dr. Samuel H. Preston—*Older Male Mortality and
Cigarette Smoking* (1970). Now we are happy to add to our
Population Monograph Series still another study of human
mortality sponsored by IPUR—this one by Dr. Robert D.
Retherford.

Dr. Retherford has tackled a facet of the precipitous mortality decline that has aroused the curiosity of everybody who has
thought about it but which has seldom been seriously investigated. This is the widening disparity in survival between men
and women. In Sweden in the latter half of the eighteenth

century, the average annual death rate for males was 28.6 per 1000, and for females 26.3 per 1000. The male excess was 8.6 percent of the female rate. In 1967 the rates were 11.0 and 9.3, respectively; the male excess had climbed to 17.8 percent. A similar change has occurred in other advanced countries and is now occurring in less developed nations.

The consequences of this change are numerous. Not the least of them is the numerical disparity of men and women at older ages and its effect on marital chances. Although more males are born than females, subsequent mortality turns this surplus into a deficit in the later ages—a deficit that has increased historically. As a result, given monogamous marriage, a high proportion of older women are forced to be unmarried. By 1970 in the United States, at ages 50 to 59, there were two unmarried women to every unmarried man, and at ages 60 to 69 there were nearly three.

In the present study, the author is not so much concerned with the consequences of the widening sex difference as he is with its causes. Using data from three countries for the period 1910 to 1965, he has parceled out the relative contributions to the trend made by alterations in the age structure, changes in causes of death, increases in cigarette smoking, reduction in the age at marriage, elimination of occupational hazards, and other factors. Some changes have tended to lessen the sex-disparity in mortality, others to increase it, but the net effect is to increase it substantially in all three countries. In developing his methods of assessing relative causation and in stating the reasoning underlying various hypotheses, the author has done more than present his statistical findings: he has advanced the theory of the sex-difference in mortality. The result, I believe, is the most comprehensive study of the subject yet made.

Kingsley Davis

International Population and Urban Research
Institute of International Studies
University of California, Berkeley
November 21, 1974

Acknowledgments

In carrying out this study, I received valuable guidance and suggestions from Professors Kingsley Davis, Nathan Keyfitz, and Samuel Preston. I am especially grateful to Kingsley Davis for numerous thoughtful suggestions on both content and style. Nathan Keyfitz raised, and encouraged me to solve, several important methodological problems. Samuel Preston gave freely of his extensive knowledge of sex mortality differentials, without the benefit of which my coverage of the topic would have been less complete. Special thanks are also due Jan Seibert, editor of this series, whose editorial suggestions have produced a much more readable and better organized text than the original. I am grateful to the editors of *Demography* for permission to reuse material from "Tobacco Smoking and the Sex Mortality Differential," which appeared in their May 1972 issue.

A grant to the Department of Demography at Berkeley from the Ford Foundation supported a substantial portion of this study. Many incidental expenses were covered by another grant to the Department of Demography from the National Center for Health Services Research and Development (8T01 HS00059), and by a grant to the Institute of International Studies at Berkeley from the Ford Foundation. An institutional grant to the East-West Population Institute from USAID supported the latter stages of the study.

R.D.R.
Honolulu, Hawaii
April 1974

The
CHANGING
SEX
DIFFERENTIAL
in
MORTALITY

1 Introduction

General mortality has improved rapidly in the twentieth century within the Western world. On the whole, however, women have benefited more than men. Summary measures of the sex mortality differential, covering all ages and causes of death, have widened. In the United States, for example, male and female expectations of life at birth rose from 48.5 and 52.0 years in 1910 to 66.9 and 73.9 years in 1965, increases of 38.0 and 41.1 percent respectively. The sex mortality differential, as measured by the female-male difference in life expectancy at birth, widened from 3.6 to 7.0 years over the same period, an increase of 94.5 percent.[1] Although not every European or New World country equalled the United States' dramatic increase in the female-male difference in life expectancy over this period, all showed some increase.

Perhaps the most important social cost of the widening mortality gap between the sexes stems from increasingly feminine sex ratios at the older ages and the related high incidence of widowhood. In the United States between 1910 and 1965, the life-table population sex ratio in the 60+ age group fell from .91 to .77 (male/female sex ratio at birth of 1.05). Over the same period the expectation of widowed life for husbands aged 23 and wives aged 21 who never divorce or remarry after

---

[1] Figures are rounded from more detailed values in Chapter 3. The base data are discussed in Appendix A, and the life table method in Appendix B. The base data for 1910 pertain only to the Death Registration Area.

death of spouse rose from 11.4 to 13.3 years for wives and fell from 7.8 to 4.6 years for husbands [Retherford, 1973]. Other notable costs are higher rates of paternal orphanhood, higher economic costs stemming from excess male mortality at the ages of maximum earning power, and greater burdens of male sickness and ill-health than would have obtained had male mortality declines kept up with female declines [Preston, 1970b:1-3]. Collectively, these undesirable consequences confer considerable social as well as scientific significance to analyses of the causes of widening sex mortality differentials, a significance which is heightened by the rapidly growing proportion of the aged within the total population.

Some initial insight into the causes of the widening sex mortality differential can be gained from examining the trend in sex differentials in age-specific mortality rates. To continue with the example of the United States, Table 1 shows that between 1910 and 1965 male-female differences in age-specific mortality declined sharply below age 5, remained fairly static at ages 5-49, and increased sharply above age 50, suggesting that mortality changes below age 5 tended to decrease the female-male difference in life expectancy, that mortality changes at ages 5-49 had little effect, and that mortality changes above age 50, therefore, accounted for virtually all of the increase.

In view of these age patterns, what might we expect to be the causes of death primarily responsible for the increases in the female-male difference in life expectancy? To answer this question it is necessary to distinguish between two levels of causes. The first level is the immediate medical causes of death, classified according to the International Classification of Diseases (ICD). The second level refers to more external factors, such as smoking, the effects of which cut across and are felt through the ICD causes of death.

Of the ICD or immediate medical causes, one of the first to consider is maternal mortality, since declines in mortality from this cause benefited females exclusively and clearly contributed

Table 1

**MALE-FEMALE DIFFERENCES IN AGE-SPECIFIC
MORTALITY RATES, UNITED STATES, 1910 AND 1965**

(rate per thousand)

Age	1910	1965
0	28.4	6.2
1-4	1.4	0.2
5-9	0.2	0.1
10-14	0.1	0.2
15-19	0.4	0.8
20-24	0.5	1.2
25-29	0.4	1.0
30-34	1.0	0.8
35-39	1.9	1.1
40-44	2.4	1.9
45-49	3.1	3.2
50-54	3.1	5.9
55-59	4.5	9.7
60-64	6.1	14.3
65-69	6.0	20.6
70-74	7.9	26.1
75-79	12.2	28.7
80-84	12.3	29.4
85+	10.4	17.6

Source: Computed from data discussed in Appendix A.
   Base data for 1910 are for the Death Registration Area only.

to the increase in the female-male difference in life expectancy.
But how important was maternal mortality in relation to other
causes? We have already seen that for ages 5-49, contributions
from all causes to the increase in the sex mortality differential
must have been proportionately very small. Because of these
small contributions, and because virtually all childbearing also
takes place within this age range, we can further reason that the

contributions of maternal mortality must also have been small. A more substantial maternal mortality contribution is of course possible if negative contributions from other causes operated partially to offset it. For example, the decline in mortality from industrial accidents, which benefited males almost exclusively, undoubtedly operated in this way.

As shown in Table 1, mortality changes in the 0-4 age group apparently tended to decrease the female-male differential in life expectancy. It seems likely that infectious and parasitic diseases, which accounted for most of the mortality declines in this age group, were primarily responsible for this effect. As mortality from these causes in the 0-4 age group declined toward zero, differences between male and female mortality rates from these causes also declined. In fact, since mortality from infectious and parasitic diseases declined greatly at other ages as well, it seems likely that the overall effect of mortality trends from these causes was to decrease the female-male difference in life expectancy, partially offsetting the overall increase.

If mortality trends above age 50 account for most of the increase in the female-male difference in life expectancy, then the ICD causes of death most responsible, since they account for most of the deaths above age 50, must almost certainly be cardiovascular-renal diseases and cancer. In the United States in 1960, cardiovascular-renal diseases and malignant neoplasms accounted for 66.1 and 15.3 percent respectively of total life-table deaths above age 50. Only 18.6 percent stemmed from other causes [US, HEW, PHS, 1968:44].

Beyond the immediate medical causes of death, what external factors might have contributed to the increases in the female-male difference in life expectancy? One factor of demonstrated importance is the increase since 1900 in per capita cigarette consumption, which has been concentrated among males and has worked to elevate mortality rates, particularly from cancer, the degenerative lung diseases (mainly chronic bronchitis and

emphysema), and cardiovascular diseases [Preston, 1970b].
Other relevant variables are working conditions, the distribution
of the population by marital status, and—mainly through their
effects on cardiovascular diseases—diet, body weight in relation
to height, exercise, and stress.

The present study elaborates a set of decomposition techniques by which to quantify the age-cause contributions to
the increase in the sex mortality differential and thereby to
determine precisely the relative importance of the epidemiological factors and some of the external factors already mentioned. Earlier explanations of the trend in the sex mortality
differential, with one notable exception [Enterline, 1961],
have not comprehensively exploited epidemiological data, no
doubt largely because of the lack of a method for easily sum-
marizing their import.

Following a review of the relevant literature in the next
chapter, the basic decomposition technique is explained in
Chapter 3 and applied in Chapters 3 and 4 to decompose, by
age and ICD cause of death, changes in two summary measures
of the sex mortality differential, the female-male difference in
life expectancy and the male-female difference in the age-
standardized death rate, over the period 1910 to 1965. A
modification of the method allows decomposition of the sex
mortality differential at each date as well. Three developed
countries form the focus: the United States (all races), England
and Wales, and New Zealand (excluding Maoris). In Chapter 5
the analysis is extended one step beyond the immediate medical
causes to assess the effects of fertility changes on the sex
mortality differential. In Chapters 6 and 7 it is further extended
to assess quantitatively the effects of two still-less immediate
external factors, smoking and marital status, the effects of
which cut across ICD cause of death categories. The effects of
these external factors are also decomposed by age and ICD
cause of death and the results integrated with the earlier age-
cause analysis of Chapters 3 and 4. Unfortunately the effects of

such relevant external variables as diet, body weight in relation to height, exercise, and stress are not considered in these chapters, because the detailed mortality data required to incorporate them into the analysis are not available.

2 Review of the Literature on Sex Mortality Differentials

A large number of animal studies suggest that inferior male longevity prevails almost without exception throughout the animal kingdom. Hamilton [1948] reviewed approximately sixty studies encompassing about seventy-five species and found inferior male longevity in almost every case. Represented were nematodes, crustaceans, insects, arachnids, reptiles, birds, and fish, as well as mammals.

Stolnitz [1956] surveyed the available data pertaining to sex mortality differentials (SMDs) in man. He oriented his discussion around two commonly made observations: (1) that sex differentials in age-specific mortality favor females in most countries at all ages, the exceptions normally involving the reproductive ages, and (2) that SMDs have been increasing over time. He found that exceptions to the first observation have been surprisingly frequent and have by no means been completely restricted to the reproductive ages. In fact, among nineteenth century European populations, reversals in SMDs by age were most frequent in the 7-17 age group. Exceptions have been less frequent in countries and periods showing higher levels of economic development, a fact which supports the observation that SMDs have been increasing over time.

Because mortality is very low at the ages where males often enjoy an advantage, the absolute differences between male and female mortality rates at these ages are small relative to those at the older ages, where females enjoy a large advantage. Hence when expectation of life is used in place of age-specific survival ratios, a very different picture emerges. As Stolnitz points

out, consistently higher female longevity has been far more
common than higher female age-specific survival ratios. Since
the 1840s, superior female longevity has been almost universal
in the West, the one clear exception being Ireland, where higher
male longevity over an appreciable range of ages was encountered
during the 1920s. Since 1930, no Western life table on record
shows a higher male life expectancy at any age to 70, and the
available data for non-Western Europe suggest that consistently
greater female longevity has also obtained for this region since
the same date. On the other hand, Stolnitz concludes from the
data that higher male life expectancy at some ages was fairly
frequent, though by no means the rule, in non-Western Europe
before World War I and in Latin America-Africa-Asia up until
the 1950s. El-Badry [1969] has noted that in India, Pakistan,
and Ceylon, male life expectancy at birth exceeded that of
females until at least the early 1960s (his data go no further).
An investigation of these exceptions is worth pursuing in subsequent studies.

Stolnitz's trend data show that in nearly every part of the
West, SMDs have been increasing persistently since about
World War I. In non-Western Europe they have been increasing
since about 1900. In the rest of the world changes in the differentials before the mid-1950s were rather irregular, but
examination of more recent data shows that since that time
SMDs have been on the increase in most of these countries, too.

In addition to Stolnitz's age analysis, there is a small literature
on the causes of death that enter into SMDs. Ciocco [1940b]
computed sex differentials in crude death rates from various
causes for the United States white population in the death
registration area in 1930. He found that circulatory diseases
showed by far the highest differential. Respiratory diseases
were second, with a differential about two-thirds as large. He
also examined a detailed list of 69 causes, obtained by picking
from the 1930 International Classification of Diseases those
causes which showed at least 1000 male or 1000 female deaths

in 1930. Males had higher rates for 74 percent of these causes, leading Ciocco to comment that "the higher mortality of the males is not general but limited to certain causes of death only."

Moriyama and Woolsey [1951] focused in more detail upon changes in the SMD for cardiovascular-renal diseases in the United States over the period 1920 to 1947. They found that among white males aged 35-64, cardiovascular-renal mortality actually increased, in contrast to marked reductions among white females in the same age group. For these same males, mortality from all other causes combined decreased. A breakdown of the cardiovascular-renal category showed that the increase in the SMD for this category was most marked for diseases of the heart, less so for chronic nephritis (kidney inflammation), and inconsequential for cerebrovascular lesions (strokes).

Dorn [1961] examined the increased mortality from chronic respiratory diseases (primarily bronchitis and emphysema) over the period 1930 to 1960. For these diseases, as well as for lung cancer, mortality rose for both sexes, but more steeply for males. On the other hand, mortality from the infectious respiratory diseases (mainly tuberculosis and pneumonia) declined for both sexes over this period.

Enterline [1961] introduced a new methodology for obtaining cause contributions to increases in male/female mortality ratios of age-standardized mortality rates. Between 1920 and 1960 in the United States, the largest increases in these ratios occurred in the 15-24 and 45-64 age groups. Enterline found that trends in death rates for tuberculosis, maternal mortality, and motor vehicle accidents were primarily responsible for increases in the 15-24 age group. Cancer of the lung, cancer of the uterus, coronary heart disease, and diseases associated with high blood pressure were important causes for increases in the 45-64 age group. These causes made themselves felt through declines in female death rates from tuberculosis, maternal mortality, cancer of the uterus, and diseases associated with

high blood pressure, and increases in male death rates from
motor vehicle accidents, lung cancer, and coronary heart disease.

In the United States between 1952 and 1967, the trend in
mortality for men was upwards for most age groups beginning
with 15-19 [US, HEW, PHS, 1971]. The most prominent
causes accounting for this increase were lung cancer, chronic
bronchitis, emphysema, cardiovascular diseases, cirrhosis of
the liver, and motor vehicle accidents. Over the same period
the trend in mortality for women was downwards at all ages
except 85 and over.

HYPOTHESES ABOUT THE DETERMINANTS
OF SEX MORTALITY DIFFERENTIALS

The approximately sixty animal studies, cited earlier, which
showed almost universal inferior male longevity in the animal
kingdom, suggest that this inferior longevity is due primarily
to biological differences between the sexes. However, biological
sex differences affect the SMD differently under different sets
of environmental conditions, so that for the SMD at a given date
the effects of these two sets of factors are in fact inextricably
intertwined. It is therefore meaningless to ask how much of the
SMD at a particular time is biologically caused and how much
environmentally caused. This is not to deny, however, that
inferior male longevity obtains under most commonly occurring sets of environmental conditions.

For the increases in human SMDs over the past fifty years,
however, it is clear that the genetic code varies too slowly for
biological differences between the sexes to have contributed
significantly. Changes in the environment must therefore have
been responsible. Nevertheless, since the effects of environmental changes on the SMD are mediated through biological
differences between the sexes, comprehension of the mechanisms

involved requires an understanding of both.

The point that biological differences cannot have initiated recent increases in SMDs has not always been fully appreciated in the literature. For example, Madigan [1957:208-209], in his well-known study of the trend in the SMD between 1900-1909 and 1950-1954 among Roman Catholic religious brother-hoods and sisterhoods, found that although sociocultural stresses were greatly equalized between the two sexes in his study population, the trend in the SMD was rather similar to that which occurred in the general population. He concluded that biological factors were more important than sociocultural factors in explaining the trend in the SMD.

The environmental or external factors usually mentioned as importantly influencing changes in the SMD are working conditions, health technology, smoking, diet, body weight in relation to height, exercise, and stress.

With regard to working conditions, we find that during the last century and the early years of this century, when working conditions were poor and the range of employment available to women was restricted, occupational risk was thought to account for a large part of the SMD [Martin, 1951:297-298]. If this is true, then, as noted earlier, subsequent improvements in working conditions, which have worked predominantly to the benefit of males, may have operated partially to offset increases in the SMD from other causes. On the other hand, the increased male disadvantage in motor vehicle accidents may have acted to wipe out any such effects of declining occupational mortality and to produce a net positive contribution of accidents as a whole to increases in the SMD. We shall attempt in the next two chapters to resolve these ambiguities regarding the net effect of accidents.

Two major respects in which the health technology variable has worked to the relative benefit of females have also been noted by Enterline [1961] in the study summarized earlier. The first is the decline in maternal mortality, which has naturally worked to the exclusive benefit of females. The other major development is the improved detection and treatment of cancer of the female reproductive organs. Mortality from cancer of the reproductive organs is very low for males, compared to that for females, so that males have had only minor benefit from the improvements in its detection and treatment.

Changes in proportionate mortality, i.e., changes in the relative importance of causes of death, represent a third way, subtle but important, in which the health technology variable has worked to the relative benefit of females. In particular, deaths from the degenerative diseases, for which SMDs are large, are now weighted more heavily than previously.

Cigarette smoking is an obvious candidate to account for part of the increase in the SMD for at least three major reasons: (1) per capita cigarette consumption has risen dramatically since the beginning of the century [US, HEW, PHS, 1956b: 107-111] ; (2) a much higher proportion of men smoke than of women [*ibid.*; Hammond, 1966] ; and (3) mortality rates for cigarette smokers are dramatically high, compared to those for nonsmokers [US, HEW, PHS, 1964b and 1967; Hammond, 1966] .

Enterline [1960:139ff] made note of all three of the above points and concluded that increases in cigarette smoking must have accounted for a substantial part of prior increases in the SMD. He also showed that for eight low mortality countries in 1950, per capita cigarette consumption for both sexes combined correlated highly with the SMD, as measured by the male/female mortality ratio of age-standardized mortality rates in the 45-64 age group.

Hammond [1966] later published mortality data by smoking status for females as well as males. The data were from a continuing study of smoking in relation to the death rates of one million men and women in the United States, carried out under the auspices of the American Cancer Society. In Chapter 6 we examine these data in detail and use them to quantify the effect of smoking on the SMD.

The remaining external variables usually mentioned as important affecting changes in the SMD are diet, body weight in relation to height, exercise, and stress. These are thought to operate primarily by raising male mortality from coronary heart disease (common heart attack), relative to female mortality from this cause.

Coronary heart disease (CHD) is almost always caused by atherosclerosis of the coronary arteries supplying the heart muscle, i.e., by fatty degeneration of the coronary artery walls [Ad Hoc Com., 1961:133-136]. Here we have a clear instance where biological differences between the sexes play an important mediating role between environmental factors and ultimate mortality. A substantial number of studies show that females are protected from atherosclerosis until menopause by estrogen hormones [Wuest *et al.*, 1953; Rivin and Dimitroff, 1954; Stamler *et al.*, 1956 and 1963; Giersten, 1965]. Because of the prophylactic effects of estrogens on atherosclerosis, any environmental change which accelerates atherosclerosis will work to the relative detriment of males. Trends in smoking habits, diet, body weight in relation to height, exercise levels, and stress levels appear to have worked in this way.

Auerbach *et al.* [1965] offer evidence that the greatly increased CHD mortality from smoking is in fact due primarily to smoking-induced acceleration of atherosclerosis. Hence we may conclude that the effect of smoking on the SMD is due not only to the fact that men smoke and inhale more than women, but also to the fact that among those who smoke and inhale equal amounts, men suffer greater acceleration of atherosclerosis than women.

The definitive study of the effects of diet on CHD was the National Diet-Heart Study [1968], carried out under the auspices of the American Heart Association. The salient findings were in basic agreement with a large number of earlier studies: saturated fats (mainly of animal origin) raise serum cholesterol; unsaturated fats (mainly of vegetable origin) lower it, but with a weaker effect for the same amount of calories, and mono-saturated fats have an insignificant effect. The study also concluded that "there is overwhelming evidence that the incidence of premature CHD is strongly associated with serum cholesterol level" [1968:2].

Jolliffe and Archer [1959] have presented data which show that the average daily caloric difference between saturated and unsaturated fat intakes in 1952 was extremely high for the developed countries, compared to underdeveloped countries. It therefore seems plausible that this index has increased for developed countries in this century and that dietary trends have accounted for part of the corresponding increases in SMDs. However, given the high proportion rural and the high proportion that animal and dairy fats probably were of farm family diets in the developed countries at the turn of the century, it is also plausible that the index was as high in 1910 as in 1952. In the United States, for example, Preston [1970b:68] has noted the following changes in fat consumption between 1909 and 1952: ". . . the average daily calories per capita of food available for consumption fell from 3,540 to 3,289, while the daily calories from fats and oils rose from 1,134 to 1,305 (from 32 to 40 percent of total calories). The proportion of fat of animal origin, which is the source of dietary cholesterol, stayed approximately constant at 70 to 73 percent" [USDA, 1953]. On the whole it appears that changes in patterns of fat consumption have probably not been large enough to account for much of the increases in SMDs.

A number of studies have shown that obesity accelerates atherosclerosis and increases the incidence of CHD [Marks, 1960]. The medical experts queried by Moriyama *et al.* [1958] felt that the emergence of the slim-figure fashion in the early 1920s led to a decline in obesity among white women. Preston [1970b:64] has cited evidence that this was indeed the case and that at the same time obesity among men increased: "Medical-actuarial data for the United States show that the average weight for males of a given height at ages 25-29 increased approximately two to ten pounds between 1885-1900 and 1940. For females at the same age, however, average weight for a given height decreased by two or three pounds" [USDA, 1960:75]. Between 1955 and 1960-1962, "males at ages between 45 and 65 appeared to gain weight in almost every height-age group, with increases on the order of one to six pounds. In this period, however, females tended to gain as much as or more than males" [USDA, 1960:11]. Overall it seems possible that male-female differentials in height-weight trends have contributed measurably to increases in SMDs in this century. On the other hand, although it has been established that persons who are excessively overweight (typically 50 pounds or more) experience excess mortality, most of which is due to CHD, several other studies have shown that for smaller amounts of excess weight, there is no significant relation between weight and mortality [Keys, 1954; Buechley *et al.*, 1958]. Since only very small proportions of either sex are excessively overweight, it appears on balance that height-weight trends have probably not affected SMDs appreciably.

The experts queried by Moriyama *et al.* [1958] also felt that markedly different dietary habits had developed among men and women, paralleling the slim-figure trend and benefiting females relative to males with regard to the incidence of CHD. Unfortunately, trend data on saturated and unsaturated fat intake are not available for each sex separately, so that the importance for the SMD of male-female differentials in dietary habits remains somewhat conjectural.

The trend toward more sedentary lives, as crudely evidenced by large increases in proportion urban, suggests that exercise declines may have accounted for part of the increase in the SMD, again primarily by having acted to increase mortality from CHD. For example, in the United States in 1900 41.7 percent of employed males worked on farms and 17.6 percent in white collar jobs. By 1960 the corresponding percentages for these categories were 8.5 and 35.4 [Preston, 1970b:65].

Fox and Skinner [1964] extensively reviewed the literature on the effects of exercise on cardiovascular health. Unfortunately there have been no definitive studies in this area, so the present summary of their review is necessarily somewhat lengthy. A substantial number of studies from this literature approached the problem by comparing male mortality in two or more occupations characterized by varying levels of physical activity. In the few studies in which smoking was controlled, the incidence of and mortality from CHD clearly varied inversely with degree of physical activity. Even in studies where no relevant variables were controlled, this inverse relation still held in most cases.

The effects of exercise have also been studied by comparing athletes and nonathletes. The results of long-term studies of athletes do not consistently show that they have lower rates of CHD in later life, but most of these studies did not control for exercise, smoking, diet, and body weight in later life. Fox and Skinner found it provocative (though not conclusive, because of small samples) that athletes who continued vigorous exercise into middle and old age had very low incidence of CHD relative to nonathletes.

The few autopsy studies that have been done showed that the extent of ischemic myocardial fibrosis associated with CHD was inversely related to the degree of physical activity, where the latter variable was again measured by last-stated occupation. Ischemic myocardial fibrosis refers to the development of scars of fibrous connective tissue in areas of the heart muscle that have insufficient blood supply. Large localized scars are usually the healed end results of major infarctions (heart attacks). Small multiple scars develop less perceptibly. A myocardial infarct is an area of dying or dead tissue in the heart muscle that develops when the arterial blood supply to that area is suddenly interrupted. Such interruptions are usually caused by embolisms. An embolism is an obstruction of a blood vessel by a piece of foreign matter, such as a blood clot or air bubble, that is too large to pass through it. Athero-sclerosis increases the incidence of embolisms because the deposit of hard fatty substances on the coronary artery walls narrows the blood channels and because chunks of these deposits sometimes break off and themselves are a source of obstructing matter.

In one of the major autopsy studies reported by Fox and Skinner, cases showing ischemic myocardial fibrosis were selected by eliminating 100 cases (out of 500) in which causes of such fibrosis other than lack of exercise might have occurred [Morris and Crawford, 1958:1485]. Cases manifesting such CHD-related clinical conditions as hypertension, diabetes, and peptic ulcer were thus omitted, but it is not clear to what extent other relevant environmental variables, particularly smoking, were taken into account. The fibrotic lesions were divided into two main groups, the first being the large discrete patch, over 1.5 cm in one dimension, often solitary, commonly transmural, and presumably the healed end result of a major infarction. The second form consisted of small multiple scars. The results showed that healed infarcts were associated with higher degrees of occupation-related physical activity and that the large fibrous patches were more closely related to the degree of physical inactivity than the small scars. In this same study, however, as well as in others, inverse correlation between degree of coronary atherosclerosis (with the exception of complete or near-complete occlusion) and degree of physical activity was either statistically insignificant or completely lacking. These studies, though in Fox and Skinner's opinion not extensive enough to be definitive or conclusive, suggest that although exercise does seem to reduce the incidence of ischemic myo-cardial fibrosis, particularly from major infarctions, it apparently does not accomplish this by significantly reducing atherosclerosis.

Fox and Skinner found the literature regarding the effect of exercise on serum cholesterol levels to be particularly confusing and inconsistent. However, to my mind, the lack of a significant correlation in this regard seems consistent with the findings of the above autopsy studies, which showed that exercise is not significantly correlated with atherosclerosis.

Another study reviewed by Fox and Skinner found that daily endurance exercise significantly reduced serum triglycerides, another blood fraction recently implicated in atherogenesis. Triglycerides are produced mainly from carbohydrates, whereas serum cholesterol is produced mainly from animal fats. The triglyceride effect of exercise seems inconsistent with the above autopsy findings that exercise is uncorrelated with coronary atherosclerosis. However, the physical activity of most of the occupations classified as active in these studies almost certainly was not sufficient to be termed endurance exercise. For this same reason, the effects on average mortality and the SMD via declines in exercise-induced triglyceride reduction have probably been minor.

An experimental study on dogs found that yet another effect of regular endurance exercise was the development of auxiliary vascularization of the heart muscle, which if it occurs in humans as well, probably reduces the destructive capabilities of embolisms and produces higher recovery rates from infarctions. To me it appears likely that this mechanism constitutes one of the primary beneficial effects of exercise in relation to CHD. But it is difficult to say whether exercise declines in this century have been steep enough to make this effect of exercise on average CHD mortality very important.

In sum, the literature suggests that exercise does reduce mortality from CHD. The physiological mechanisms involved, however, are not well understood. The association of atherosclerosis with exercise seems to be minor, and of other likely mechanisms, auxiliary vascularization of the heart muscle seems most important. Because the shift out of farming has produced declines in average exercise levels that probably have been more marked for males than for females, the adverse effects of exercise declines on CHD, though probably small in comparison to those of increased cigarette consumption, have undoubtedly worked to the relative detriment of males. Exercise declines have probably adversely affected mortality from causes other than CHD as well, but I am unaware of evidence indicating that any such effects importantly influence the SMD.

It is frequently alleged that life is progressively more rushed and stressful in modern societies, and that this added stress is another external factor aggravating CHD, especially for males. Smith [1967], Marks [1967], and Caffrey [1967] have extensively reviewed the literature on this subject. They found much conflicting evidence, a good deal of which is no doubt again due to most studies failing to control for smoking and other external factors when comparing groups and occupations characterized by different degrees of stress. Although on balance the evidence does suggest that stress elevates serum cholesterol levels and accelerates atherogenesis, the conflicting evidence indicates that this effect is small. As Preston [1970b:67] has pointed out, the most convincing evidence of the importance of stress would be epidemics of CHD at times of long-term national stress. But during World War II, for example, CHD death rates often fell, particularly in occupied countries [Malmros, 1950; Strom and Jensen, 1951]. Another difficulty is the lack of any firm evidence that the average level of psychological stress has risen appreciably since the beginning of the century. The best-known demographic study of the effects of stress on the SMD is Madigan's study of Roman Catholic brotherhoods and sisterhoods, cited earlier, among whom it was found that, although sociocultural stress was greatly equalized between the sexes, the trend in the SMD was rather similar to that which occurred in the general population [Madigan, 1957]. It should be added that many of the problems with the literature on stress and mortality stem from the lack of adequate measures of stress.

The only study to date that has attempted quantitatively to order external variables according to the size of their contributions to changes in the SMD was done by Preston [1968], who considered cigarette smoking, diet, exercise, and stress. Preston designed a new measure of excess older male mortality, relative to both younger male and older female mortality, and then, for each of seventeen European and New World countries, computed an average value of this measure over the period 1950 to 1963. Using a multiple regression technique, he then determined the contribution of each external variable to this average value of excess mortality in each of the seventeen countires. On average, the smoking contribution was by far the largest, and of the remaining three variables, only the diet contribution was of any importance.

Although Preston's smoking and dietary measures were precise, the measures of national exercise and stress levels were necessarily indirect because of the paucity of available data. Stress was measured by average per capita consumption, by percentage of the male labor force employed outside of agriculture, forestry, fishing, and hunting, and by change in the above percentage between 1910 and 1960. Exercise was measured by percentage of male labor force aged 45-64 employed in tertiary industries. Since it is questionable whether these measures reflect very accurately the phenomena they are intended to measure, Preston's conclusions on the contributions of stress and exercise must be regarded as suggestive but not conclusive.

A hypothesis, quite different from those so far discussed, of how environmental and genetic variables interact to affect the SMD has been called the "impaired lives hypothesis." Preston has reexamined it recently [1970a].

Raymond Pearl [1939] and Mortimer Spiegelman [1968] have contended that low death rates in early life permit the survival of many "impaired lives" which die at a faster rate later on. On the other hand, Kermack, McKendrick and McKindlay [1934] have adduced evidence showing, for an 80-year period in England and Wales, exactly the opposite. Cohort death rates at older and younger ages were in fact *positively* related; death rates at an older age would not decline until death rates at a younger age in the same cohort had declined. Whatever "weeding out" of genetically susceptible organisms occurred, its visibility was obscured by quantitatively more important factors operating in the opposite direction.

> . . . Sex differences in the composition of the 23rd pair of chromosomes have often been alleged to be deleterious to a male's chances of survival. Consequently, a relaxation of the mortality environment might well permit the survival of many more male "impaired lives" than female.

To test the impaired lives hypothesis, Preston computed, for 27 Swedish cohort life tables, the coefficient of partial correlation between $_5m_{55}$ (the death rate in the cohort at ages 55 to 59) and l_{55} (the proportion of the birth cohort which survived to age 55), holding constant the mortality level at the time when $_5m_{55}$ was recorded (the period expectation of life at age 5 was employed for this purpose). The value of this coefficient was -.727 for males and -.902 for females. The negative relationships are the opposite of those predicted by the genetic hypothesis. Thus Preston's findings support the view that the impaired lives effect, insofar as it exists, tends, at least in the short run, to be obscured by quantitatively more important factors operating in the opposite direction and has little effect on SMDs.

3 Methodology

AN ILLUSTRATION: THE
UNITED STATES, 1910-1965

The probable reasons for increases in the female-male difference in life expectancy in the United States during the twentieth century were discussed in Chapter 1, and the likely contributions to these increases from mortality changes in certain age groups and from certain of the immediate ICD medical causes of death were mentioned. This section develops a decomposition technique to assess quantitatively these age-cause contributions. The decomposition of the change in the female-male difference in life expectancy (e_0) in the United States over the period 1910 to 1965 is used to illustrate the technique. The comparison of results to those inferred in Chapter 1 continues the discussion from that chapter.

Male and female expectations of life at birth in the United States increased from 48.46 and 52.01 years in 1910—a 3.55 year difference—to 66.88 and 73.87 years in 1965—a 6.99 year difference—an increase of 3.43 years in the sex mortality differential (corresponding figures in Chapter 1 were rounded to tenths of a year). The percentaged contributions to this increase of 3.43 years, from mortality changes from each immediate medical cause of death in each age group, are shown in Table 2.

Table 2 was calculated as follows. The procedure for deriving age contributions was to form a set of mortality rates using 1910 mortality levels for all but one age group for which

Table 2

AGE-CAUSE CONTRIBUTIONS TO $\Delta(e_0^f - e_0^m)$, UNITED STATES, 1910-1965[a]

Age[b]	Cause of Death[c]									Residual[d]	Total
	I-P	C-R	NEO	RESP	DIG	MAT	INF	ACC	OTH		
0-19	5.6	0.8	0.1	-5.3	-8.9	1.2	-5.3	-2.5	-4.0	-3.1	-21.3[e]
20-39	-0.4	3.8	2.3	-2.2	1.1	11.6	0.0	-8.7	2.9	0.6	11.1
40-59	-6.5	20.5	9.8	-1.4	2.0	1.2	0.0	-8.2	1.0	2.1	20.4
60-79	-0.1	15.9	8.1	7.5	2.4	0.0	0.0	-1.4	1.2	9.0	42.6
80+	0.1	-0.5	0.4	1.8	0.4	0.0	0.0	0.3	1.3	0.4	4.1
Residual[d]	-1.0	1.8	-0.2	0.7	0.3	0.0	0.0	-0.3	0.3	41.3	43.0
Total	-2.2	42.3	20.6	1.1	-2.6	14.1	-5.3	-20.8	2.6	50.3	100.0
											(3.43)

[a] $\Delta(e_0^f - e_0^m)$ denotes the change in the female-male difference in life expectancy. Entries in the table denote percentages of the total change of 3.43 years (in parentheses at the lower right) that are due to mortality changes in each age-cause category. A negative sign indicates that an age-cause-specific mortality change worked to change the overall SMD in a direction opposite to that of the overall change.

[b] Although shown here by 20-year age groups, the orginal mortality data and calculations on which the table is based were grouped in conventional abridged life table age intervals.

[c] Appendix A contains the ICD list numbers for the cause categories, which are abbreviated in column heads as follows:

I-P = Infectious-parasitic diseases
C-R = Cardiovascular-renal diseases
NEO = Neoplasms, both malignant and benign
RESP = Respiratory diseases (including infant pneumonia)
DIG = Digestive diseases (including infant diarrhea)

MAT = Maternal mortality
INF = Certain diseases of early infancy (excluding pneumonia and diarrhea)
ACC = Accidents, poisonings, violence
OTH = All other causes

[d]Residuals, calculated so that rows and columns add to marginal totals, are mathematical artifacts of the decomposition procedure and do not represent empirical interactions between causes (see Appendix C).

[e]Because of rounding errors, rows and columns do not always add exactly to marginal totals.

the 1965 level was used. A new value of the sex mortality differential (SMD) was calculated using this set of mortality rates, with value SMD*. Then (SMD* - SMD_{1910}) is interpreted as the component of the change in the SMD due solely to mortality changes in that age group. Cause contributions were derived similarly, by varying mortality for one cause category at a time, and age-cause contributions by varying mortality for one age-cause category at a time. Residuals were calculated so that rows and columns added to marginal totals. Finally, percentaging gave the results shown.

The methodology of varying one thing at a time, if it may be called that, is well established. For example, Kitagawa [1955:1178] used it as one of several procedures by which to decompose changes in crude rates; Keyfitz [1968b:189-193] used it to decompose changes in the mean age in the stable population into mortality, fertility, and residual components; and Davis [1965b:50] used it to separate the growth of cities into general population growth, true urbanization (increases in proportion urban), and residual components.

Although the residual contributions in Table 2 are large, thereby muddying its interpretation, nevertheless the relative order of importance of the various age-cause contributions is clear. The table verifies most of the inferences drawn in Chapter 1 about the ages and causes of probable importance. Mortality changes at the older ages, particularly ages 60-79, indeed contributed the greater part of the increase in the female-male difference in life expectancy (F-M difference in e_0), and the contribution from mortality changes at the youngest ages, 0-19 in the table, was actually negative, as predicted.

Most of the negative 0-19 age contribution stemmed from the respiratory, digestive, infancy, and accidents categories. Except for accidents, the infectious disease components of these categories probably accounted for most of this negative contribution, even though the 0-19 infectious-parasitic contribution itself was positive. The total infectious-parasitic contribution for all ages, however, was negative as expected, although not strikingly so.

From the small changes in M-F differences in age-specific mortality rates in the childbearing ages over the period 1910-1965 (Table 1), it was inferred in Chapter 1 that the contributions to the increase in the F-M difference in e_0 from mortality changes at these ages must have been relatively small. It was further reasoned that the maternal mortality contribution must therefore also have been small, unless negative contributions from other causes operated partially to offset it. The decline in mortality from industrial accidents, which benefited males almost exclusively, was pointed out as an undoubtedly offsetting cause. Table 2 validates these inferences. The 20-39 age contribution was small, only 11.1 percent of the total increase. The 20-39 maternal mortality contribution of 11.6 percent was slightly larger, and this was indeed made possible by a negative 20-39 accidents contribution of -8.7 percent. Of course, the accidents category in Table 2 contains much more than industrial accidents, but it does seem likely that the industrial accidents component accounted for most of the negative contribution from this category. The positive contribution from motor vehicle accidents to increases in SMDs, noted by Enterline [1961] and mentioned in Chapter 2, was apparently more than offset by this negative contribution from the industrial accidents component. (For reasons of time and expense, a finer cause breakdown was not introduced in the decomposition to verify this interpretation unequivocally.) Overall, trends in mortality from accidents, poisonings, and violence produced a substantial negative contribution of -20.8 percent.

As predicted, the cardiovascular-renal and neoplasms contributions to the increase in the F-M difference in e_0 were by far the largest, and they were concentrated at ages above 40. This finding is consistent with the fact that male-female differences in age-standardized mortality rates from the cardiovascular-renal diseases and neoplasms increased markedly over the period, whereas for the other cause categories in the table, these male-female differences either increased slightly, or, more commonly, decreased.

The 60-79 respiratory contribution of 7.5 percent was also substantial, being almost as large as the neoplasms contribution for that age group. The importance of the 60-79 respiratory contribution no doubt stems from the increased incidence among males of the chronic respiratory diseases associated with smoking, mainly chronic bronchitis and emphysema (application of the decomposition technique with a finer cause breakdown would be necessary to confirm this statement unequivocally). However, because of negative respiratory contributions at ages below 60, caused by declines to near-zero levels in age-sex-cause-specific rates (and therefore also in M-F differences between these rates) from the infectious respiratory diseases, the overall respiratory contribution was only slightly positive.

The analysis so far has focused on the decomposition of changes in the SMD over time. The method can be modified easily to decompose also the SMD at a particular time point. Instead of letting age-sex-cause-specific rates vary one at a time from their beginning values to their end values in time, we take the rates for a given year and let them vary one at a time from their male values to their female values. (There is no reason why the reverse procedure could not be used alternatively— letting rates vary one at a time from their female values to their male values.) Table 3 shows such decompositions for the United States in 1910 and 1965.

Tables 2 and 3 complement each other. Table 2 shows that trends in the infectious-parasitic, digestive, infancy, and accidents categories acted to reduce the F-M difference in e_0, while Table 3 shows that these same cause categories fell sharply as percentages of the total SMD. With regard to positive contributions, Table 2 shows that the cardiovascular-renal and

Table 3

AGE-CAUSE CONTRIBUTIONS TO ($e_0^f - e_0^m$), UNITED STATES, 1910 AND 1965

Date	Age		Cause of Death									Residual	Total
		I-P	C-R	NEO	RESP	DIG	MAT	INF	ACC	OTH		
1910	0-19	-0.4	0.2	0.2	9.3	13.5	-1.1	12.2	8.9	7.0	0.5	50.3
	20-39	4.0	-0.7	-2.5	3.0	-0.3	-10.6	-0.0	21.5	-1.8	-0.3	12.3
	40-59	8.4	2.9	-8.4	4.2	0.7	-1.1	-0.0	13.5	0.8	0.1	21.2
	60-79	1.6	8.2	-2.3	-0.7	0.1	0.0	0.0	3.2	1.5	0.2	11.7
	80+	0.0	1.0	-0.1	-0.4	-0.0	0.0	-0.0	-0.1	0.4	-0.0	0.8
	Residual	0.1	0.2	0.1	0.1	0.0	0.0	-0.0	1.0	0.0	2.1	3.6
	Total	13.7	11.8	-12.9	15.4	14.1	-12.7	12.2	48.0	7.9	2.5	100.0
												(3.55)
1965	0-19	0.1	0.1	0.3	0.9	0.3	-0.1	3.9	4.5	0.8	0.0	10.9
	20-39	0.0	1.4	-0.3	0.2	0.2	-0.4	0.0	10.1	0.3	0.0	11.5
	40-59	0.4	17.0	0.3	1.4	1.5	-0.0	0.0	4.6	0.7	0.6	26.6
	60-79	0.5	21.2	5.7	3.3	1.3	0.0	0.0	1.6	1.0	3.7	38.4
	80+	0.0	1.3	0.7	0.5	0.1	0.0	0.0	0.1	0.3	0.3	3.2
	Residual	0.0	2.1	0.1	0.1	0.0	0.0	0.0	0.2	0.0	6.9	9.4
	Total	1.1	43.2	6.8	6.4	3.4	-0.5	3.9	21.1	3.1	11.5	100.0
												(6.99)

neoplasms categories acted to increase immensely the SMD, while Table 3 shows that these categories rose sharply as percentages of the total SMD. On the other hand, the respiratory and "other" categories in Table 3 declined in proportionate importance between 1910 and 1965, even though in Table 2 they contributed positively to the absolute increase in the SMD over the period. We shall attempt later to resolve this apparent inconsistency (see discussion below relating to the respiratory and digestive contributions in Tables 6 and 7).

In Table 3 the negative neoplasms contributions to the F-M difference in e_0 in 1910 are consistent with the low per capita cigarette consumption and the high mortality rates existing at that time from cancer of the female reproductive organs. Maternal mortality in 1910 accounted for only -12.7 percent of the F-M difference in e_0, indicating that in the United States during the twentieth century, maternal mortality apparently never accounted for very much of this measure of the SMD. By 1965 the maternal mortality contribution was almost negligible. A rather surprising finding is that accidents accounted for almost half of the F-M difference in e_0 in 1910. This finding corroborates Martin's [1951:287] view, mentioned in Chapter 2, that occupational risk probably accounted for a large part of the SMD at the beginning of the century. The concentration of the 1910 accidents contribution at the working ages 20-59 supports the inference that industrial accidents were mostly responsible for the importance of the accidents category at that time.

THE M-F DIFFERENCE IN THE AGE-STANDARDIZED DEATH RATE AS AN ALTERNATIVE SMD MEASURE

Although the analysis thus far has utilized the F-M difference in e_0 to measure the sex mortality differential, it is apparent that a wide variety of measures could fruitfully be used. The F-M difference in e_0 is an especially attractive measure because its common-sense meaning in terms of length of life is immediately obvious to the layman as well as to the professional demographer. For application of the decomposition techniques used in this study, a second measure—the M-F difference in the age-standardized death rate (SDR)—is also particularly convenient because of its mathematical properties, one of which is that the residual contributions in the decompositions are uniformly zero.

The proof that the residuals are always zero for decompositions utilizing the SDR is straightforward. Consider the change over time in the M-F difference in the SDR. Let P_x represent the standard population by age, expressed as a set of proportions, and M_{xi} the age-cause-specific mortality rate for cause i at age x. By definition the M-F difference in the SDR is

$$\text{SDR}^m - \text{SDR}^f = \sum_x \sum_i P_x M_{xi}^m - \sum_x \sum_i P_x M_{xi}^f \qquad (3.1)$$

We therefore have that

$$\text{SDR}^m - \text{SDR}^f = \sum_x \sum_i P_x (M_{xi}^m - M_{xi}^f) \qquad (3.2)$$

$$= \sum_x \left\{ \sum_i P_x (M_{xi}^m - M_{xi}^f) \right\} \qquad (3.3)$$

$$= \sum_i \left\{ \sum_x P_x (M_{xi}^m - M_{xi}^f) \right\} \qquad (3.4)$$

Equations (3.2) to (3.4) give the M-F difference in the SDR analyzed as a sum of age-cause contributions, as a sum of age marginal contributions, and as a sum of cause marginal contributions. There are no residual terms.

The decomposition of the change over time in the M-F difference in the SDR gives rise to a similar set of equations.

$$\Delta(SDR^m - SDR^f) = \sum_x \sum_i P_x \, \Delta(M^m_{xi} - M^f_{xi}) \qquad (3.5)$$

$$= \sum_x \left\{ \sum_i P_x \, \Delta(M^m_{xi} - M^f_{xi}) \right\} \quad (3.6)$$

$$= \sum_i \left\{ \sum_x P_x \, \Delta(M^m_{xi} - M^f_{xi}) \right\} \quad (3.7)$$

Equations (3.5) to (3.7) give the sum of the age-cause contributions, the sum of the age marginals, and the sum of the cause marginals. Again there are no residuals.

It is evident that for this measure of the SMD, decompositions could in fact be calculated directly from equations (3.2) to (3.7) without going through the equivalent and more generally applicable but more cumbersome procedure of varying mortality in one age-cause category at a time.

In the case of the M-F difference in the SDR, the choice of a young or old standard age distribution makes a difference in the results. A young standard age distribution weights heavily the decreases in M-F differences of age-specific rates at the very young ages (Table 1), so that the M-F difference in the SDR with a young standard shows a less dramatic increase over time than it does with an old standard. Likewise, in the decomposition of the increase in the M-F difference in the SDR, the absolute values of the percentaged age-cause contributions at the young ages are larger and those at the old ages smaller with a young standard than with an old standard. Nevertheless, experimentation with the 1911 and 1961 age distributions of England and

Wales as standards shows that the relative order of importance of age-cause contributions is for the most part the same. An exception is the respiratory category. Changes in M-F differences in age-specific rates for respiratory diseases tend to be large and of opposite sign at the young and old ages (declines at the young ages and increases at the old ages) and relatively small in between, making the overall contribution from respiratory diseases abnormally sensitive to changes in age distribution.

Table 4 shows the decomposition of the change in the M-F difference in the SDR for the United States between 1910 and 1965, using as a standard the 1961 age distribution of England and Wales for both sexes. Comparison of Tables 2 and 4 shows that the decompositions using the SDR and e_0 are quite different numerically, but that the relative order of importance of age-cause contributions is again substantially the same. The presence of large residual contributions in the decompositions using e_0 of course makes precise numerical comparisons of little value.

Since for the measures of the SMD considered thus far, a shift from one to another does not appreciably alter the relative order of importance of age-cause contributions in the decompositions, to avoid needless repetition it is both possible and desirable to use only one measure in most of the subsequent analysis. Inasmuch as decompositions using the SDR contain no residuals and are considerably easier and less expensive to compute than decompositions using e_0, the M-F difference in the SDR was usually chosen. Since the 1961 England and Wales age distribution roughly reflects contemporary age distributions in developed countries, it appeared to be a more interesting standard than the 1911 age distribution, which was also considered. Therefore only the 1961 distribution was used thenceforth.

An alternative standard might have been the stable age distribution corresponding to age-specific mortality and fertility

Table 4

AGE-CAUSE CONTRIBUTIONS TO $\triangle$(SDR^m - SDR^f), UNITED STATES, 1910-1965[a]

Age	Cause of Death									Total
	I-P	C-R	NEO	RESP	DIG	MAT	INF	ACC	OTH	
0-19	0.4	0.0	0.1	-4.2	-6.8	0.6	-3.5	-1.5	-3.0	-17.8
20-39	-3.7	2.1	1.9	-2.3	0.4	7.7	0.0	-7.0	1.6	0.7
40-59	-13.4	31.2	16.6	-3.9	2.0	1.3	0.0	-13.1	0.1	20.8
60-79	-3.3	41.5	32.0	18.6	5.1	0.0	0.0	-5.3	-3.5	85.2
80+	-0.1	-1.9	5.6	7.8	1.1	0.0	0.0	1.3	-2.8	11.1
Total	-20.1	73.0	56.3	16.1	1.8	9.6	-3.5	-25.5	-7.7	100.0
										(2.42)

[a]The standard is the 1961 age distribution of England and Wales for both sexes. Between 1910 and 1965 (SDR^m - SDR^f) increased from 3.12 to 5.54 per thousand (see Table 5).

in England and Wales in 1961, rather than the actual age distribution. Stable age distributions reflect solely the long-term effects of current age-specific mortality and fertility on age distribution, so that they are independent of the past history of the actual population. Since it appears desirable that a current mortality measure reflect as little as possible of the past history of the population, the use of stable age distributions as standards seems a practice worth adopting (see, for example, Preston *et al.* [1972]). A further advantage of stable age distributions as standards is that for positive intrinsic rates of natural increase, they decrease monotonically with age. Actual populations may show irregular profiles by age, due to wars, baby booms, and other historical events. As a matter of fact, the 1961 England and Wales age distribution, used as a standard throughout much of the present study, itself declines somewhat irregularly with age. However, since 20-year age intervals are used in the decompositions throughout most of this study, the effects of these irregularities are fairly well smoothed out. It does not appear that the substitution of stable for actual age distributions would make much difference in the conclusions reached in this study. Therefore, the somewhat inappropriate choice of standards does not constitute a serious defect.

COMPARISON TO ENTERLINE'S DECOMPOSITION TECHNIQUE

It was noted in Chapter 2 that Enterline [1961] introduced a new methodology for obtaining cause contributions to increases in M/F ratios of age-standardized mortality rates. His method, with a few notational and expositional modifications, is as follows. If over a given age range we let

SDR^m = male age-standardized mortality rate

SDR^f = female age-standardized mortality rate

SDR_i^m = male age-standardized mortality rate for cause i

SDR_i^f = female age-standardized mortality rate for cause i

then we have, using the calculus of differentials, that

$$\Delta \left(\frac{SDR^f}{SDR^m} \right) \cong \sum_i \frac{SDR^f}{SDR^m} \left(\frac{\Delta SDR_i^f}{SDR^f} - \frac{\Delta SDR_i^m}{SDR^m} \right) \qquad (3.8)$$

Equation (3.8) is a sum of cause-specific contributions. Although Enterline did not do so, we can modify (3.8) to give a complete age-cause breakdown. Let P_x denote the standard age distribution, expressed as a set of proportions, and let M_{xi} denote the age-cause-specific mortality rate for cause i at ages x to x + n. Then (3.8) becomes

$$\Delta \left(\frac{SDR^f}{SDR^m} \right) \cong \sum_x \sum_i \frac{SDR^f}{SDR^m} P_x \left(\frac{\Delta M_{xi}^f}{SDR^f} - \frac{\Delta M_{xi}^m}{SDR^m} \right) \;, \qquad (3.9)$$

which is a sum of age-cause-specific contributions. I have compared this amplified version of Enterline's method with the method of varying mortality in one age-cause category at a time by using both approaches to decompose the change in the F/M ratio in SDR(40-69) over the period 1950-1965 in the United States. Corresponding percentaged age-cause contributions match up quite well, never disagreeing by more than two percentage points. Both methods result in residual contributions, since in general the calculus of differentials also gives inexact decompositions of finite changes.

It is apparent that for analysis of changes in F/M ratios of age-standardized rates, the modified Enterline approach gives results that are just as good as those obtained by the method of varying mortality in one age-cause category at a time. The advantage of the latter method, as compared to Enterline's, is that it can be used on a wide variety of measures of the SMD to which Enterline's method is not applicable, and can be used to decompose SMDs at a given time point as well as to decompose changes in SMDs over time. This advantage is only statistical, however, and does not imply a superior description of how causes combine to produce the total effect. With either method, for example, residual contributions represent mathematical, not empirical interactions (see Appendix C). The mathematical nature of the interactions reflects an artificiality which characterizes decompositions obtained by either method and makes the choice between them somewhat arbitrary.

Enterline's analysis focused on the 15-24 and 45-64 age groups, because M/F ratios of age-specific mortality rates were notably higher there than in other age groups. At first sight, the high M/F mortality ratio in the 15-24 age group seems to contradict the finding in Table 3 that the 20-39 age contribution to the F-M difference in e_0 was minor in the United States in both 1910 and 1965. The reason for this apparent discrepancy is that when mortality for both sexes is low, as it is in the 15-24 age group, M/F mortality ratios can be quite large while M-F mortality differences are necessarily small. For decompositions involving summary measures of the SMD, covering all ages and causes of death, it is the differences and not the ratios that are most relevant, since they better reflect the volume of excess male deaths. For the M-F difference in the SDR, the point is illustrated mathematically in equations (3.1) to (3.7), where the SMD and changes in it are seen to be linear functions of differences of age-cause-specific rates.

This is not to say, however, that movements in differences and ratios of age-cause-specific mortality rates are totally independent of one another. In fact, in a situation of declining mortality an increase in the M-F difference in the SDR implies a corresponding increase in the M/F ratio of the SDR. This can be seen as follows. Let k represent the M/F ratio of the SDR. Then

$$\Delta(SDR^m - SDR^f) = \overline{SDR^f}\Delta k + \overline{k\text{-}1}\ \Delta SDR^f \qquad (3.10)$$

where $\overline{SDR^f}$ and $\overline{k\text{-}1}$ are simple arithmetic means, obtained by summing values at the beginning and end of the period in question and dividing by two. Since for developed countries in the twentieth century k is always greater than 1, the second term on the right is negative. Hence if $\Delta(SDR^m - SDR^f)$ is positive, then the first term on the right must also be positive— i.e., Δk must be positive.

The same reasoning holds true for increasing male-female differences in age-cause-specific mortality rates. The corresponding M/F ratios must also increase if age-cause-specific mortality is falling and the age-cause-specific k is greater than one. However, in some categories, such as automobile accidents, mortality has risen instead of fallen, in others, such as certain kinds of cancers, k is less than one, and in still others, such as infectious respiratory diseases, male-female mortality differences have fallen instead of risen. In these latter situations male-female mortality differences and ratios do not necessarily move in the same direction.

THE PROBLEM OF COMPETING RISKS

The method of varying mortality in one age-cause category at a time can be subjected to some minor modifications to bring it into line with the literature on competing risks of death. It is not quite correct to assume, as is done in Tables 2 to 4, that mortality rates and probabilities of dying from a given cause remain unchanged when mortality from another cause is deleted or reduced [see, for example, Greville, 1948; US, HEW, PHS, 1968; Chiang, 1968:Ch. 11]. At ages of rising age-specific mortality, the age-specific rate that would be observed if mortality from one cause were eliminated or reduced would be higher than that actually observed. At ages of falling age-specific mortality, it would be lower.

Chiang [1968:Ch. 11] derives formulae for evaluating the effects on the life table q's of deleting mortality from a given cause. We have the following definitions:

P_i = Pr{an individual alive at age x_i will survive the interval (x_i, x_{i+1})}

q_i = Pr{an individual alive at x_i will die in the interval (x_i, x_{i+1})}

$q_{i\delta}$ = Pr{an individual alive at x_i will die in the interval (x_i, x_{i+1}) if R_δ (the risk of dying from cause δ) is the only risk acting on the population}

$q_{i\cdot\delta}$ = Pr{an individual alive at x_i will die in the interval (x_i, x_{i+1}) if R_δ is eliminated as a risk of death}

$Q_{i\delta}$ = Pr{an individual alive at x_i will die in the interval (x_i, x_{i+1}) from R_δ in the presence of all other risks in the population}

Chiang obtains the relationship

$$q_{i\cdot\delta} = 1 - p_i^{(q_i - Q_{i\delta})/q_i} . \qquad (3.11)$$

The estimator of $q_{i\cdot\delta}$ turns out to be

$$\hat{q}_{i\cdot\delta} = 1 - \hat{p}_i^{(D_i - D_{i\delta})/D_i} , \qquad (3.12)$$

where $\hat{p}_i$ is the p_i from the unaltered life table and the D's are observed deaths. Equivalently,

$$\hat{q}_{i\cdot\delta} = 1 - p_i^{(M_i - M_{i\delta})/M_i} , \qquad (3.13)$$

where the M's are the age-specific rates.

The above equations must be altered somewhat for the purposes of the present study, since we wish not to eliminate mortality from a given cause but merely to reduce it. Let $f(x)$ denote the fraction by which the force of mortality from cause δ is reduced at age x. We assume that over the interval (x_i, x_{i+1}) $f(x)$ is constant. Let f_i denote this constant value. Following a derivation procedure which parallels Chiang's, we get

$$q_{i \cdot \delta} = 1 - p_i^{(q_i - f_i Q_{i\delta})/q_i} , \qquad (3.14)$$

where $q_{i \cdot \delta}$ now represents the probability with mortality from R_δ reduced instead of eliminated.

We estimate f_i by the fractional reduction in $M_{i\delta}$ over the period in question, $\hat{f}_i$. Then

$$\hat{q}_{i \cdot \delta} = 1 - \hat{p}_i^{(M_i - \hat{f}_i M_{i\delta})/M_i} \qquad (3.15)$$

If we denote the reduced value of $M_{i\delta}$ by $M_{i\delta}^*$, then

$$\hat{f}_i = \frac{M_{1\delta} - M_{i\delta}^*}{M_{i\delta}} , \qquad (3.16)$$

and (3.13) becomes

$$\hat{q}_{i \cdot \delta} = 1 - \hat{p}_i^{(M_i - M_{i\delta} + M_{i\delta}^*)/M_i} \qquad (3.17)$$

If $M_{i\delta}^* = 0$, (3.17) reduces to (3.13), as one would expect.

For the purposes of the present study, (3.17) provides the basis for calculating altered life tables. I have compared decompositions of the change in the F-M difference in e_0 based on this equation to decompositions based on the method of varying mortality in one age-cause category at a time and have found very close agreement between them. Rarely do two corresponding percentaged age-cause contributions differ by more than one or two percentage points; usually they differ by considerably less. Since adjustments for competing risks have little effect on results, and since they would complicate considerably the calculation and analysis of decompositions based on the SDR, they have not been incorporated in the remainder of this study.

4 Analysis of Sex Mortality Differentials by Age and Medical Cause of Death

THE UNITED STATES, ENGLAND AND WALES, AND NEW ZEALAND COMPARED

It is of some interest to go beyond the example of the United States in Chapter 3 to see if patterns are peculiar to it or apply generally to mortality trends in other developed countries. Two additional countries were chosen for this purpose: England and Wales, and New Zealand (excluding Maoris). The choice of these countries hinged primarily on ready availability of data. Other countries with historical age-cause mortality data suitable in quality and format for the analysis made here include Australia, Italy, Norway, and Sweden [see Preston *et al.*, 1972].

Earlier work by Ledermann [1964:77ff] suggests that the developed countries fall into four groups, in terms of the pattern of their sex differentials in cause-specific death rates between ages 45 and 65: the United States, Great Britain, Canada, Australia, and New Zealand, with similar SMDs; 21 other developed countries clustering into three separate and distinct groups. Hence the mortality experience of the three countries examined here does not necessarily typify all developed countries, but it probably does represent fairly well the experience of the English-speaking group.

Table 5 shows the changes in the M-F difference in the SDR to be analyzed. Corresponding changes in the F-M difference in life expectancy are also shown but are not subsequently analyzed. In all three countries the sex mortality differential

Table 5

TIME TRENDS IN THE SDR AND e_0, UNITED STATES, ENGLAND AND WALES, AND NEW ZEALAND

(SDR as rate per thousand)

		SDR			e_0		
		M	F	M-F	M	F	F-M
US	1910	24.30	21.18	3.12	48.46	52.01	3.55
	1930	19.74	16.74	3.00	57.31	60.70	3.39
	1950	15.24	10.74	4.51	65.30	70.92	5.62
	1965	14.49	8.95	5.54	66.88	73.87	6.99
EW	1910	23.77	19.54	4.23	49.35	53.38	4.03
	1930	18.95	14.90	4.04	59.02	63.27	4.25
	1950	15.61	11.02	4.59	66.57	71.32	4.75
	1965	14.63	8.85	5.78	68.53	74.79	6.26
NZ	1910	17.69	14.75	2.94	60.27	63.12	2.85
	1930	15.75	13.22	2.53	64.36	67.26	2.90
	1950	14.01	10.64	3.37	68.39	72.22	3.83
	1965	13.97	8.98	4.98	68.78	74.65	5.87

aValues for England and Wales and New Zealand labelled 1910 are actually for 1911. Values for the United States in 1910 and 1930 pertain only to the Death Registration Area. For further discussion see Appendix A.

changed little between 1910 and 1930, then increased rapidly to give a large net increase over the entire period 1910-1965. The net increase in the M-F difference in the SDR is examined first, then the subperiod trends.

Table 6 shows both the decompositon of the change in the M-F difference in the SDR over the period 1910-1965, and the decomposition of this measure of the SMD at each of the two dates, 1910 and 1965 (for reasons of space, only the age and cause marginal contributions of the decompositions are presented). The general pattern is much the same in all three countries. Trends in the infectious-parasitic, infancy, accidents, and "other" categories acted to reduce the SMD in all three countries. With regard to positive contributions, cardiovascular-renal diseases and neoplasms contributed immensely to the increase in the SMD in all three countries. The age contributions are concentrated at the older ages, in line with the overwhelming importance of cardiovascular-renal diseases and neoplasms.

Examination of the M-F differences in age-cause-specific rates (not shown) shows that the relatively small infectious-parasitic contributions for New Zealand stemmed from two offsetting trends: (1) the large decrease over the period in the M-F difference in age-specific mortality from infectious-parasitic diseases during the first year of life, and (2) the large increases in M-F differences in age-specific mortality from this cause category at ages 15-29 and 70+. In the United States and England and Wales the first trend was somewhat more pronounced and the second much less pronounced. Neither country experienced the large negative M-F differences in age-specific mortality from infectious-parasitic diseases at ages 15-29 and 70+ that New Zealand did in 1910. The 1965 values of these differences, on the other hand, were fairly similar in all three countries. It is in fact generally true of all the cause and age contributions that the decompositions for the three countries were more similar in 1965 than in 1910. This trend toward epidemiological uniformity can be related to the

Table 6

CAUSE AND AGE CONTRIBUTIONS TO (SDRm - SDRf), 1910 AND 1965,
AND TO Δ(SDRm- SDRf), 1910-1965, UNITED STATES,
ENGLAND AND WALES, AND NEW ZEALAND

		United States			England and Wales			New Zealand		
		1910	1965	1910-65	1910	1965	1910-65	1910	1965	1910-65
Cause Contributions	I-P	18.2	1.5	-20.1	13.9	1.2	-33.3	2.5	1.1	-.9
	C-R	41.1	55.0	73.0	19.2	47.1	123.2	24.7	53.0	93.5
	NEO	-21.1	12.7	56.3	-3.2	19.7	82.1	-3.7	13.6	38.5
	RESP	4.1	9.3	16.1	20.7	22.2	26.2	16.6	15.9	14.7
	DIG	6.0	4.2	1.8	6.2	2.2	-8.7	1.9	2.4	3.2
	MAT	-7.8	-.2	9.6	-3.6	-.2	9.2	-6.4	-.2	8.8
	INF	4.9	1.3	-3.5	3.2	.9	-5.3	3.3	.9	-2.7
	ACC	42.2	12.7	-25.5	15.2	4.8	-23.6	34.2	9.3	-26.4
	OTH	12.4	3.6	-7.7	28.4	2.1	-69.8	26.8	4.1	-28.6
	T	100.0	100.0	100.0	100.0	100.0	100.0	100.0	100.0	100.0
		(3.12)	(5.54)	(2.42)	(4.23)	(5.78)	(1.55)	(2.94)	(4.98)	(2.05)
Age Contributions	0-19	20.2	3.6	-17.8	14.1	2.8	-28.1	10.2	3.5	-6.2
	20-39	8.1	4.9	.7	5.5	2.1	-7.2	-.1	4.4	10.8
	40-59	28.2	24.9	20.8	22.3	17.1	2.7	21.3	18.2	13.9
	60-79	36.3	57.6	85.2	45.7	62.9	109.8	47.2	59.9	78.2
	80+	7.3	9.0	11.1	12.3	15.1	22.8	21.4	14.0	3.4
	T	100.0	100.0	100.0	100.0	100.0	100.0	100.0	100.0	100.0
		(3.12)	(5.54)	(2.42)	(4.23)	(5.78)	(1.55)	(2.94)	(4.98)	(2.05)

virtual disappearance of substantial short-term fluctuations over time in mortality and to the general decline of mortality differences among European and New World nations that has come about from the rapid diffusion of health technology during this century [Arriaga and Davis, 1969:234-235].

In England and Wales and New Zealand in 1910, contributions from the "other" category were proportionately larger and those from the cardiovascular-renal category proportionately smaller than corresponding contributions in the United States. This suggests a geographic difference in diagnostic fashions. That is, the percentages suggest that many deaths classified as cardiovascular-renal in the United States in 1910 would have been classified as senility and ill-defined conditions (one component of the "other" category) in England and Wales and New Zealand. The large negative neoplasms contribution for the United States in 1910, which also exceeded those of the other two countries, suggests that the same may have been true for this cause category. This hypothesis gains added weight when the detailed age breakdown of the "other" contribution to the 1910 differential is examined (not shown). The 60-79 and 80+ age groups account almost entirely for the inflation of the "other" category for England and Wales and New Zealand in 1910. It is in these age groups that the cardiovascular-renal and neoplasms contributions are concentrated. Moriyama [1948:537-545] and Woolsey and Moriyama [1948:1247-1273] have suggested that even for the United States there may have been some shifts in diagnoses from other disease groups into the circulatory group. The results presented here suggest that this trend was relatively smaller for the United States than for England and Wales and New Zealand. The sex differential in the proportion of deaths from senility and ill-defined conditions was in fact noticeably greater in England and Wales and New Zealand than in the United States in the first decades of the century, whereas by 1965 country differences were negligible [UN, 1962:70-73].

Diagnostic shifts may also account partly for respiratory contributions for England and Wales and New Zealand considerably exceeding those of the United States in the decompositions of the SMD at each date in Table 7. Although deaths from acute and chronic bronchitis, which are part of the respiratory category, are often infectious in origin, they are also frequently associated with myocardial degeneration. It has been asserted that many deaths assigned to bronchitis in England and Wales and New Zealand would elsewhere be assigned to heart disease [Preston *et al.*, 1972:112-115]. The sex differential in mortality from bronchitis is in fact much larger for England and Wales and New Zealand than for the United States or for non-English-speaking low-mortality countries [UN 1962:113; Preston, 1970a:9].

The decompositions in Table 6 illustrate a methodological point that came up earlier in connection with Tables 2 and 3. Although, for example, respiratory diseases contributed substantially to the increase in the M-F difference in the SDR, the proportion of the M-F difference in the SDR that this category accounted for at the two end dates either increased very little or, in the case of New Zealand, even declined slightly. This is at first confusing. However, if the M-F difference in the SDR widens over the period, while the proportion accounted for by the respiratory category remains approximately unchanged, then it is clear that the unpercentaged contribution from this category must also increase. Given the representations of this measure of the SMD and changes in it over time in equations (3.1 to 3.7), it is in fact easy to show that the condition for a zero contribution by a given cause to the change is that the percentage for that cause vary inversely as the total unpercentaged SMD between the beginning and the end dates. The same condition applies to the age marginals and to the detailed age-cause contributions. To take another category, the digestive, as a specific example, the percent contribution from this category to the SMD in the United States in 1965 is .7 of its contribution in 1910. The unpercentaged value of the total

Table 7

CAUSE CONTRIBUTIONS TO (SDR^m - SDR^f), 1910, 1930, 1950, AND 1965,
AND TO Δ(SDR^m - SDR^f), 1910-1930, 1930-1950, AND 1950-1965,
UNITED STATES, ENGLAND AND WALES, AND NEW ZEALAND

		I-P	C-R	NEO	RESP	DIG	MAT	INF	ACC	OTH	Total
US	1910	18.2	41.1	-21.1	4.1	6.0	-7.8	4.9	42.2	12.4	100.0 (3.12)
	1930	9.8	44.8	-11.6	10.2	6.2	-7.1	4.2	38.3	5.3	100.0 (3.00)
	1950	6.3	56.4	5.0	5.0	4.7	-.7	2.2	16.2	4.9	100.0 (4.51)
	1965	1.5	55.0	12.7	9.3	4.2	-.2	1.3	12.7	3.6	100.0 (5.54)
	1910-30	231.6	-53.6	-259.6	-150.6	1.8	-24.9	24.6	140.9	190.0	100.0 (-.12)
	1930-50	-.6	79.6	38.2	-5.4	1.8	12.0	-1.6	-28.1	4.0	100.0 (1.50)
	1950-65	-19.6	48.8	46.4	28.3	1.7	2.0	-3.0	-2.6	-1.9	100.0 (1.03)
EW	1910	13.9	19.2	-3.2	20.7	6.2	-3.6	3.2	15.2	28.4	100.0 (4.23)
	1930	10.4	29.8	4.5	19.8	6.4	-2.8	3.4	13.5	15.1	100.0 (4.04)
	1950	6.3	39.6	14.6	19.7	4.5	-.5	1.7	6.6	7.5	100.0 (4.59)
	1965	1.2	47.1	19.7	22.2	2.2	-.2	.9	4.8	2.1	100.0 (5.78)
	1910-30	91.9	-213.0	-170.8	40.7	.5	-20.5	.4	51.0	319.8	100.0 (-.18)
	1930-50	-24.0	112.2	90.7	18.9	-9.4	16.6	-10.4	-45.5	-49.1	100.0 (.54)
	1950-65	-18.2	76.2	39.1	31.8	-6.9	1.3	-2.2	-2.1	-19.0	100.0 (1.19)
NZ	1910	2.5	24.7	-3.7	16.6	1.9	-6.4	3.3	34.2	26.8	100.0 (2.94)
	1930	6.2	26.3	3.1	21.7	4.3	-6.5	3.6	30.4	10.7	100.0 (2.53)
	1950	6.3	47.1	9.9	9.3	4.2	-1.2	1.9	13.3	9.3	100.0 (3.37)
	1965	1.1	53.0	13.6	15.9	2.4	-.2	.9	9.3	4.1	100.0 (4.98)
	1910-30	-20.8	14.6	-46.6	-15.4	-13.6	-5.7	1.3	57.7	128.5	100.0 (-.40)
	1930-50	6.3	109.9	30.2	-28.2	3.6	14.7	-3.4	-38.4	5.2	100.0 (.84)
	1950-65	-9.7	65.3	21.5	29.4	-1.2	2.1	-1.3	.8	-6.9	100.0 (1.61)

SMD in 1965 is 1.8 times its former value. But .7, though close to .6, the inverse of 1.8, is nevertheless somewhat greater, so that the contribution of the digestive category to the change is small but positive.

It is noteworthy that each percentaged age-cause contribution to the change in the SMD in Table 6 is either greater or less than, but never in between, the two corresponding age-cause contributions to the SMD at the beginning and end of the period in Table 7. The explanation of this pattern is as follows. We denote

$C_{xi}^{(1)}$: the proportionate contribution of the x-ith age-cause category to SMD at time 1

$C_{xi}^{(2)} : a_{ix} C_{ix}^{(1)}$: the proportionate contribution of the x-ith age-cause category to SMD at time 2, where a_{ix} is defined as $C_{ix}^{(2)} / C_{ix}^{(1)}$

C_{xi}^{*} : the proportionate contribution of the x-ith age-cause category to $\triangle$SMD.

Then

$$C_{xi}^{*} = C_{xi}^{(1)} \left[\frac{(a_{xi})\,(SMD^{(2)})\text{-}SMD^{(1)}}{SMD^{(2)}\text{-}SMD^{(1)}} \right] = C_{xi}^{(2)} \left[\frac{SMD^{(2)}\text{-}SMD^{(1)}\,/a_{xi}}{SMD^{(2)}\text{-}SMD^{(1)}} \right] \quad (4.1)$$

From examination of (4.1) we see that, for $0 < SMD^{(1)} < SMD^{(2)}$,

$$\left. \begin{array}{l} \text{If } a_{xi} = 1, \text{ then } C_{xi}^{*} = C_{xi}^{(1)} = C_{xi}^{(2)} \\[2mm] \text{If } a_{xi} > 1, \text{ then } C_{xi}^{*} > (C_{xi}^{(1)} \text{ or } C_{xi}^{(2)}) \\[2mm] \text{If } a_{xi} < 1, \text{ then } C_{xi}^{*} < (C_{xi}^{(1)} \text{ or } C_{xi}^{(2)}) \end{array} \right\} \quad (4.2)$$

Statement (4.2) is usually valid also for decompositions based on e_0, but not always. In Tables 2 and 3 of the previous chapter, the cardiovascular-renal contributions are exceptions. For decompositions based on e_0, the computational procedures are such that equation (4.1) is only approximately satisfied.

ANALYSIS OF CHANGES OVER THE THREE SUBPERIODS 1910-1930, 1930-1950, AND 1950-1965

Table 5 showed that the M-F difference in the SDR actually decreased in all three countries over the period 1910-1930, then increased thereafter to give a large net gain over the entire period 1910-1965. The $\triangle$SMD decompositions in Table 7 show the cause contributions to these changes over the three periods. In the United States the small decrease in the SMD over the period 1910-1930 was due to the unpercentaged negative contributions to $\triangle$SMD from primarily the infectious-parasitic, accidents, and "other" categories outweighing the positive contributions from primarily the cardiovascular-renal, neo-plasms, and respiratory categories and, to a lesser extent, the maternal mortality category. The other two countries show somewhat different patterns. In England and Wales for 1910-1930, the unpercentaged respiratory contribution was negative. The corresponding contributions in the United States and New Zealand were positive. In New Zealand, the unpercentaged infectious-parasitic contribution was positive. The corresponding contributions in the United States and England and Wales were negative. The exceptional character of infectious-parasitic contributions to the New Zealand SMD in 1910 was noted earlier. Again, the predominance of the "other" contribution in England and Wales and New Zealand is very noticeable and may be due to diagnostic shifts.

Table 8

AGE CONTRIBUTIONS TO (SDR^m - SDR^f), 1910, 1930, 1950,
AND 1965, AND TO Δ(SDR^m - SDR^f), 1910-1930, 1930-1950, AND
1950-1965, UNITED STATES, ENGLAND AND WALES,
AND NEW ZEALAND

		0-19	20-39	40-59	60-79	80+	Total
	1910	20.2	8.1	28.2	36.3	7.3	100.0 (3.12)
US	1930	13.4	4.7	28.3	43.8	9.9	100.0 (3.00)
	1950	5.6	5.0	28.3	51.6	9.5	100.0 (4.51)
	1965	3.6	4.9	24.9	57.6	9.0	100.0 (5.54)
	1910-30	192.8	93.7	24.5	-153.0	-58.0	100.0 (-.12)
	1930-50	-10.0	5.6	28.3	67.3	8.8	100.0 (1.50)
	1950-65	-4.9	4.3	10.1	83.9	6.6	100.0 (1.03)
	1910	14.1	5.5	22.3	45.7	12.3	100.0 (4.23)
EW	1930	10.1	3.6	22.9	51.3	12.1	100.0 (4.04)
	1950	4.2	1.6	21.4	59.0	13.8	100.0 (4.59)
	1965	2.8	2.1	17.1	62.9	15.1	100.0 (5.78)
	1910-30	102.4	47.5	10.0	-77.1	17.2	100.0 (-.18)
	1930-50	-40.0	-13.5	10.4	116.5	26.5	100.0 (.54)
	1950-65	-2.6	4.1	.4	77.8	20.2	100.0 (1.19)
	1910	10.2	-.1	21.3	47.2	21.4	100.0 (2.94)
NZ	1930	9.5	4.6	17.6	44.7	23.5	100.0 (2.53)
	1950	6.0	2.9	16.8	63.6	10.7	100.0 (3.37)
	1965	3.5	4.4	18.2	59.9	14.0	100.0 (4.98)
	1910-30	14.9	-29.9	44.2	62.5	8.3	100.0 (-.40)
	1930-50	-4.4	-2.5	14.3	120.7	-28.1	100.0 (.84)
	1950-65	-1.9	7.5	21.2	52.3	20.9	100.0 (1.61)

A striking aspect of the decompositions for the period
1910-1930 is the large size of the percentaged contributions.
The unpercentaged contributions to the change over the
period 1910-1930 approximately offset one another and are
therefore large in comparison to the total change. The 1910-
1930 age contributions in Table 8 show similar exaggeration

effects. In the United States, the negative unpercentaged contributions of the 0-19 and 20-39 age categories are quite large in relation to the total change. The same is true for the positive unpercentaged contributions of the 60-79 and 80+ age categories. Again England and Wales depart somewhat from the United States pattern, and New Zealand scarcely fits at all.

It is apparent that because of the small total changes and attendant exaggeration effects, cross-country comparisons of $\triangle$SMD decompositions for the period 1910-1930 in Tables 7 and 8 are not very illuminating. On the other hand, the $\triangle$SMD decompositions for the periods 1930-1950 and 1950-1965 in the same tables seem to jibe quite well with those for the entire period 1910-1965 in Table 6. This is in part because the total changes are larger for these two periods, so that exaggeration effects intrude less. One noteworthy aspect of the decompositions over these two subperiods is the considerable reduction of the relative size of the "other" contribution compared to that of the period 1910-1930. This suggests that the bulk of the diagnostic shifts out of the "other" category (assuming that this indeed occurred) took place between 1910 and 1930.

The decompositions of the M-F difference in the SDR at each of the four dates, 1910, 1930, 1950, and 1965, show that the "other" contribution was indeed approximately halved between 1910 and 1930. The trends in the proportionate composition of this measure of the SMD by age and cause are quite consistent over time for all three countries. This consistency is more visible here than in the decompositions of changes because of the absence of exaggeration effects. The trends have been remarked upon earlier. The infectious-parasitic, infancy, accidents, and "other" contributions became smaller over each successive period while the cardio-vascular-renal and neoplasms contributions became larger. The proportionate contribution from the respiratory and digestive categories did not change much. Maternal mortality contributed negatively at all four dates, but by 1965 its contribution was negligible. Note that New Zealand's un-usually small infectious-parasitic contribution in 1910 had already assumed a more normal size by 1930 in relation to the other two countries. The most noteworthy trend in the age marginals is, as before, the regular decrease in the im-portance of the 0-19 contribution and the almost as regular increase in the importance of the 60-79 contribution.

A partial explanation of the anomalous decrease in the SMD over the period 1910-1930 might be that the effects of increases in cigarette smoking, which, as we shall see in Chapter 6, accounted for almost half of the SMD in 1962 and three quarters of its increase between 1910 and 1962, had not yet begun to be felt by 1930. Cigarette consumption per capita in the United States was quite low before World War I. It rose suddenly during that war, slightly more than doubling between 1915 and 1918, and then slightly more than doubled again between 1918 and 1930 [US, HEW, 1956b:107]. It seems likely that this rapid spread of the cigarette habit took place predominantly among men in their late teens and twenties, so that the bulk of those who acquired the cigarette habit between 1915 and 1940 did not begin to feel significantly the effects of cigarette smoking on coronary heart disease, lung cancer, and chronic respiratory diseases until after age 40, which for these men was subsequent to 1930.

5 Fertility, Maternal Mortality, and the Sex Mortality Differential

Fertility is seldom considered as a cause of death. Nevertheless it has a two-fold effect on mortality and the sex mortality differential: directly through maternal mortality and indirectly through nonmaternal causes of death. Indirect effects occur when a birth to a surviving mother works to change her longevity from what it would have been without that birth.

INDIRECT EFFECTS OF FERTILITY ON THE SMD

The available evidence on indirect effects is mostly in the form of parity differentials in mortality from all nonmaternal causes lumped together, typically after age 45. The difficulty is that these differentials can be interpreted either as causal or as due to selection. A causal interpretation is as indicated above for indirect effects—the birth changes the mother's longevity. A selection interpretation implies that, ceteris paribus, the genetically more robust women, who would have lived longer anyway, are more successful in achieving large families than the less robust. With selection, mortality differentials by parity may occur even in the absence of true (i.e., causal) indirect effects. Of course, one should also take into account fertility and mortality differentials between social groups, and processes of social as well as genetic selection. When this is done the problem of sorting out causal from selection effects becomes even more formidable.

The selection interpretation seems quite plausible, but there is also at least one causal mechanism by which survived pregnancies and births act to reduce mortality at later ages. A number of studies, cited earlier in Chapter 2, show that estrogen hormones significantly slow the development of atherosclerosis, the principal cause of coronary heart disease. Since an extra birth increases the fraction of the reproductive age span spent in a hyperestrogenic state during pregnancy and lactation, it reduces the risk of death from coronary heart disease at later ages. Since coronary heart disease accounts for a large proportion of female deaths after age 45, this effect could be significant.

Past studies of the effect of fertility on mortality have focused primarily on the indirect effects of fertility on female longevity. Freeman [1935] obtained records for 1,614 married women from a genealogical series and statistically controlling for year of birth (before 1750, 1750-1799, and 1800-1824) and age at marriage, found a small positive correlation between length of life after age 45 and the number of offspring. Dorn and McDowell [1939] used Australian vital statistics in a similar approach to the problem, controlling for year of marriage and age at marriage. Married women who died after age 45 between 1909 and 1928 were classed into thirty groups, corresponding to six 10-year year-of-marriage categories, beginning with 1845-1854 and ending with 1895-1904, and five 5-year age-at-marriage categories, beginning with 15-19 and ending with 35-39. Within each of these thirty categories the relationship between age at death and number of children per 100 married women was examined. With the exception of women married in the earliest of the six time periods, 1845-54, a positive relationship was found in almost every case.

Kiser *et al.* [1968:13] computed by parity the proportion of native white women aged 45-54 in the United States in 1950 surviving to 1960 and found that women with five or more children had higher survival ratios than those with fewer than five.

Childless women were an exception, having higher survival ratios than women with children. The ratios ranged from .920 to .985.

Kitagawa and Hauser [1973], in their Matched Records Study of the United States in 1960, found that the mortality of ever-married white women, standardized for age and education, was greater for women with no children or one child (by 7 and 4 percent respectively above the average) and for women with 5 or 6 children (5 percent above the average) or 7 or more children (14 percent above the average). The authors speculate that many women with one or no children are subfecund because of health problems which also lead to high mortality. However, they note that the higher rates of mammary cancer for women who do not bear and nurse children suggest that at least some of the explanatory factors are causal. The control for socioeconomic status via education does not appear to explain the disagreement between the positive association of mortality with parity at the higher parities and the negative association found by Kiser *et al.* Since parity in 1960 was inversely related to socioeconomic status, which was in turn inversely related to mortality, Kitagawa and Hauser would probably have shown even higher mortality at the high parities had socioeconomic status not been controlled.

In sum, the observed associations between fertility and nonmaternal mortality appear weak and contradictory. No firm statements can be made about causal effects, but these are probably quite small, since selection no doubt accounts for part of the observed relationships. The indirect effects of fertility on the sex mortality differential are therefore probably also very small.

DIRECT EFFECTS OF FERTILITY ON THE SMD

Tables 9 and 10 present for the United States, England and

Wales, and New Zealand over the period 1910-1965 the base data on fertility and maternal mortality needed to compute direct effects of fertility, through maternal mortality, on the sex mortality differential. Since in all three countries fertility was already relatively low by 1910, it seemed desirable to include additional data for an earlier year in which fertility was substantially higher. Data for England and Wales in 1861 were available and were included for this purpose.

Table 9 shows that the total fertility rate declined in all three countries until 1930, increased between 1930 and 1950, then dropped off slightly between 1950 and 1965 except for England and Wales, where it continued to increase. Since most age-specific rates at the older reproductive ages declined after 1930 as well as before, the post-1930 increase in the total fertility rate stemmed almost entirely from increases in age-specific rates between ages 15 and 35.

Age-specific maternal mortality rates, in the sense of maternal deaths/female population (D/P), generally declined over the same periods, as shown in Table 10. The exceptions are rather surprising, because they occurred in the United States and New Zealand between 1910 and 1930 at ages where fertility declined. The apparent contradiction is resolved by the italicized rates in the same table, which show that age-specific maternal mortality, in the sense of maternal deaths/births (D/B), rose between 1910 and 1930. Maternal mortality (D/P) can increase and fertility decrease if maternal mortality (D/B) rises fast enough.

The increases in maternal mortality (D/B) before 1930 are startling. Not only did they occur in all three countries between 1910 and 1930, but also in England and Wales over the earlier period 1861 to 1910. For the United States between 1917 and 1930, the increase in maternal mortality (D/B) has been noted

Table 9

AGE-SPECIFIC FERTILITY RATES AND TOTAL FERTILITY RATES,
UNITED STATES, ENGLAND AND WALES, AND NEW ZEALAND[a]

(rate per 1000)

		15-19	20-24	25-29	30-34	35-39	40-44	TFR
	1910	64.1	193.3	186.7	140.3	103.8	40.9	3,645.0
	1930	48.4	122.7	116.4	86.5	55.9	23.8	2,267.4
US	1950	82.4	198.9	165.6	102.6	51.8	15.7	3,084.2
	1965	72.2	198.8	163.9	96.1	47.2	13.8	2,960.0
	1861	27.3	154.5	224.3	217.0	181.5	100.2	4,524.0
	1910	11.9	106.7	167.5	147.5	101.8	44.0	2,897.0
EW	1930	14.9	92.8	122.7	89.4	50.8	18.9	1,946.4
	1950	22.1	126.0	135.9	89.2	48.1	15.2	2,182.4
	1965	44.8	176.3	178.1	101.5	48.4	13.4	2,812.5
	1910	20.2	115.1	170.9	156.9	113.2	52.5	3,144.4
	1930	18.2	108.1	146.3	114.6	72.7	30.6	2,452.4
NZ	1950	29.8	184.9	215.5	144.3	77.2	25.8	3,387.5
	1965	52.3	220.0	207.6	114.4	57.0	18.9	3,350.9

[a]Values for England and Wales in 1861 are actually just for England. Values
for England and Wales and New Zealand labelled 1910 are actually for 1911.
Values for the United States in 1910 (estimated) and 1930 are for the Birth
Registration Area only. Discrepancies between Total Fertility Rates and corresponding sets of age-specific rates are due to rounding errors. For further
discussion, see Appendix A.

also by Shapiro *et al.* [1968:145]. They found that the maternal
mortality rate skyrocketed during the influenza epidemic of
1919-1920, then declined almost to the pre-epidemic level. It

Table 10
AGE-SPECIFIC MATERNAL MORTALITY RATES, UNITED STATES, ENGLAND AND WALES, AND NEW ZEALAND, BY FEMALE POPULATION AND BIRTHS[a]

(rate per 100,000 female population)   (rate per 100,000 births)[b]

		15-19		20-24		25-29		30-34		35-39		40-44	
US	1910	23	363	65	337	81	432	84	597	75	722	46	1,122
	1930	34	709	60	487	67	580	69	799	62	1,107	35	1,477
	1950	6	68	9	47	10	63	11	107	10	189	5	330
	1965	1	20	3	17	4	26	4	46	4	81	2	124
EW	1861	11	416	34	219	54	242	62	284	66	363	70	695
	1910	6	519	30	279	48	288	56	381	57	556	36	816
	1930	4	266	23	245	41	337	46	510	39	769	24	1,257
	1950	1	55	6	49	9	65	9	97	8	171	5	334
	1965	1	17	3	15	4	20	3	33	3	57	1	99
NZ	1910	9	452	28	245	55	320	89	564	65	573	40	754
	1930	8	422	44	411	66	449	58	504	51	701	26	856
	1950	3	114	13	68	10	48	14	95	9	119	13	510
	1965	0	0	4	16	1	7	6	51	1	24	0	0

[a]Obtained by dividing the maternal mortality rates in Table 9 (the figures used here were less rounded than those shown in Table 9 and the female population columns). fertility rates in Table 9 (the figures used here were less rounded than those shown in Table 9 and the female population columns).

[b]Values for England and Wales in 1861 are actually just for England. Values for England and Wales and New Zealand labelled 1910 are actually for 1911. Values for the United States in 1910 and 1930 are for the Death Registration Area only. For further discussion, see Appendix A.

rose again between 1927 and 1929, then declined slowly until 1936, after which time it dropped very rapidly, due to the discovery of sulfonamides, used to control puerperal infections, and the coming into general use of blood and blood substitutes for transfusions in the treatment of hemorrhage.

McKeown and Brown [1955] presented evidence suggesting that the increasing prevalence of hospital delivery may have been partly responsible for the overall increase in maternal mortality (D/B) during the latter half of the nineteenth century. Mid-century hospital deliveries were more hazardous than home deliveries because of the prevalent well-documented unhygienic conditions. Hospital deaths from puerperal infections were common. The authors cite one study which estimated mortality in a large number of confinements in all parts of Europe as 34.0 and 4.7 per thousand deliveries for hospital and home deliveries respectively. Contemporary English estimates were found consistent with these figures; there were substantial variations in the rates from one hospital to another, and in the same hospital from year to year, but with few exceptions death rates for hospital deliveries were many times greater than those for home deliveries. It is possible, of course, that because home delivery was usual at mid-nineteenth century, women with difficult pregnancies predominated among those giving birth in hospitals, and that this selective factor accounted for part of the home-hospital maternal mortality differential. Nonetheless, to the extent that unhygienic conditions were more characteristic of hospital than home deliveries, increases in the proportion of hospital births without doubt tended to increase maternal mortality.

If abortions were increasing as a proportion of total births during the two periods before 1930, they might also explain part of the increase in maternal mortality (D/B). The D/B rate would be inflated not only by the relatively high risk of dying from an abortion, but also by the lack of additional live births in the denominator of the rate corresponding to the additional maternal deaths from abortion in the numerator.

Unfortunately the 1929 Revision of the International Classification of Diseases is the first to include deaths from abortion as a separate subcategory of the overall maternal deaths category. It is therefore not possible to verify from published cause-of-death data that the proportionate importance of deaths from abortion increased over this period.

Widening class differentials in fertility, which worked to increase lower-class births as a proportion of total births, may also have contributed to increases in maternal mortality (D/B) during the latter half of the nineteenth century, given the coexistence of a class differential in mortality. In that half-century, the class difference in fertility began to widen noticeably in the industrializing countries, peaked around the turn of the century, depending on the circumstances of the particular nation, and eventually began to contract. In 1910 in the United States, for instance, the highest occupational class, the professional, had a cumulative reproductive performance, among its married women with husband present, which was 58 percent of that of the lowest class, unskilled laborers [Davis, 1965a]. On the other hand, the adverse effect of widening class fertility differentials on maternal mortality may have been more than offset by the growth of the middle class, which worked to decrease lower-class births as a proportion of total births. Despite their earlier possible importance, class fertility differentials cannot—since they peaked near the turn of the century—account for the further increases in maternal mortality between 1910 and 1930 which occurred in all three countries. On the whole, it seems likely that even during the nineteenth century the effects of widening class fertility differentials on maternal mortality were comparatively unimportant.

With the data in Tables 9 and 10 the direct effects of fertility on the sex mortality differential can be calculated by applying the decomposition methodology from Chapters 3 and 4. For the SMD in a given year, the methodology is unchanged, and the contribution of maternal mortality (D/P), calculated in Chapter 4, indicates the combined effect of fertility and maternal mortality (D/B). I have not been able to devise a satisfactory procedure to split this combined effect into two parts.

With a change in the SMD over time, however, it is possible to split the maternal mortality (D/P) contribution into two parts, one due to fertility change by itself and the other to maternal mortality (D/B) change. If we let MM_x, mm_x, and F_x represent age-specific rates for maternal mortality (D/P), maternal mortality (D/B), and fertility, then

$$MM_x = F_x mm_x \qquad (5.1)$$

(The usual practice of defining mm_x as the ratio of all maternal deaths to live births is followed here, but it should be noted that in reality not every maternal death from complications of pregnancy, childbirth, or the puerperium is associated with a live birth.) From (5.1), a change in MM_x over time can be written as

$$\Delta MM_x = \overline{mm}\, \Delta F_x + \overline{F}_x\, \Delta mm_x \qquad , \qquad (5.2)$$

where $\overline{F}_x$ and $\overline{mm}_x$ are simple arithmetic means, obtained by summing the values at the beginning and end of the period in question and dividing by two. This breakdown is of a type used by Kitagawa [1955] to decompose the difference between two crude rates. The two components in (5.2) can be regarded as changes in two separate causes of death and incorporated as such into the decompositions of changes in the SMD in Chapters 3 and 4. When this is done the maternal mortality (D/P) contributions in those decompositions are also split into two parts, one due to fertility change and the other to maternal mortality (D/B) change. The remaining age-cause contributions are unchanged.

The decompositions of changes in SMDs in Table 11 reflect the offsetting trends in fertility and maternal mortality (D/B) rates which Tables 9 and 10 showed occurred for all periods except 1950 to 1965 (since the detailed age-cause contributions from fertility and maternal mortality (D/B) are so small, they are not shown). In all three countries between 1910 and 1930, and in England and Wales between 1861 and 1930, fertility declines acted to increase the SMD while maternal mortality

Table 11

FERTILITY AND MATERNAL MORTALITY CONTRIBUTIONS TO $\triangle$(SDR^m-SDR^f), UNITED STATES, ENGLAND AND WALES, AND NEW ZEALAND

		Fertility	Maternal Mortality (D/B)	Other Causes	Total
1910-1930	US	-97.3	72.4	124.9	100.0 (-.12)
	EW	-36.6	16.4	120.2	100.0 (-.18)
	NZ	-12.9	7.4	105.6	100.0 (-.40)
1930-1950	US	-2.0	13.9	88.0	100.0 (1.50)
	EW	-0.5	17.1	83.4	100.0 (.54)
	NZ	-3.5	18.2	85.3	100.0 (.84)
1950-1965	US	0.1	1.9	98.0	100.0 (1.03)
	EW	-0.2	1.5	98.7	100.0 (1.19)
	NZ	0.1	1.9	98.0	100.0 (1.61)
1910-1965	US	3.6	5.9	90.4	100.0 (2.42)
	EW	3.9	5.2	90.8	100.0 (1.55)
	NZ	1.2	7.5	91.2	100.0 (2.05)
1861-1930[a]	EW	19.4	-10.1	90.7	100.0 (.86)
1861-1965	EW	2.1	5.1	92.9	100.0 (2.60)

[a]The values of the SDR in 1861 were 28.81 for males and 25.63 for females. The F-M difference in the SDR was therefore 3.18. For further discussion of the data, see Appendix A.

(D/B) increases had a partially offsetting effect. From 1930 to 1950 the pattern of fertility and D/B contributions was reversed, D/B declines substantially offsetting fertility increases. By 1950 maternal mortality was so low that further changes in fertility and maternal mortality between 1950 and 1965 had an almost negligible impact on the increases in the SMD.

In contrast to the relatively large fertility and maternal mortality (D/B) contributions in the 1861 to 1930 decomposition for England and Wales, those in the overall 1861 to 1965 decomposition are quite small. The reason is that the bulk of the increase in the M-F difference in the SDR over the period 1861 to 1965 occurred only after 1930 when fertility and maternal mortality contributions to the change in the sex mortality differential were unimportant, so that fertility and D/B changes from 1861 to 1930 receive little weight in the overall 1861 to 1965 decomposition. In fact, the net maternal mortality (D/P) contribution was even smaller in the 1861-1965 decomposition than in the 1910-1965 decomposition. The fertility contribution was somewhat larger but the maternal mortality (D/B) contribution somewhat smaller in the former decomposition than in the latter, reflecting the larger fertility declines and smaller maternal mortality (D/B) declines during the former period than during the latter.

DIRECT EFFECTS OF FERTILITY CHANGE ON FEMALE LONGEVITY

Since much of the literature concerning the effects of fertility on mortality deals with female longevity, using the above decomposition technique to assess the direct effects should prove interesting. Table 12 shows that fertility changes never accounted for more than ± 3 percent of the increase in female longevity over any of the three subperiods after 1910. Maternal mortality (D/B) contributions were only slightly more

Table 12

FERTILITY AND MATERNAL MORTALITY CONTRIBUTIONS TO Δe_0^f
UNITED STATES, ENGLAND AND WALES, AND NEW ZEALAND

		Fertility	Maternal Mortality (D/B)	Other Causes	Residual	Total
	US	2.7	-2.1	99.3	0.1	100.0 (8.69)[a]
1910-30	EW	1.3	-0.5	99.0	0.2	100.0 (9.89)
	NZ	3.0	-2.1	99.0	0.1	100.0 (4.14)
	US	-1.0	5.5	94.3	1.2	100.0 (10.22)
1930-50	EW	-0.2	3.1	96.3	0.7	100.0 (8.05)
	NZ	-2.0	9.4	91.7	0.9	100.0 (4.96)
	US	0.1	2.2	97.2	0.5	100.0 (2.95)
1950-65	EW	-0.3	1.7	98.2	0.4	100.0 (3.47)
	NZ	0.1	4.1	95.0	0.8	100.0 (2.43)
	US	0.3	1.9	96.4	1.4	100.0 (21.86)
1910-65	EW	0.0	1.4	97.7	0.9	100.0 (21.41)
	NZ	0.0	3.9	94.7	1.3	100.0 (11.53)
1861-1930	EW	1.2	-0.6	99.0	0.4	100.0 (20.21)
1861-1965	EW	0.2	0.7	98.0	1.1	100.0 (31.73)

[a]Female life expectancy in England and Wales in 1861 was 43.06 years. Values at later dates for the United States, England and Wales, and New Zealand were 52.01, 59.38, and 63.12 in 1910 (actually 1911 for England and Wales and New Zealand); 60.70, 63.27, and 67.26 in 1930; 70.92, 71.32, and 72.22 in 1950; and 73.87, 74.79, and 74.65 in 1965.

substantial than this over the last two periods. For the period 1910-1965 as a whole, over which the net fertility change was rather small (Table 9), the fertility contributions were negligible in all three countries. Contributions were also extremely small from 1861 to 1930, as well as for the entire 1861 to 1965 span.

The reason why fertility and maternal mortality (D/P) contributions to increases in female longevity are proportionately so much smaller than the corresponding contributions to increases in the sex mortality differential is most easily discerned by viewing all mortality changes in terms of age-standardized death rates and sex differences between them. In absolute terms, the overall declines in female standardized death rates have been vastly greater than the increases in sex differences in standardized death rates. Since the absolute contribution of changes in maternal mortality rates (D/P) to declines in female death rates or to increases in sex differences in death rates has been the same, fertility and maternal mortality changes have had a proportionately greater impact on sex differences.

6 Tobacco Smoking and the Sex Mortality Differential

Per capita cigarette consumption has risen dramatically since the beginning of the century. Mortality rates for cigarette smokers are much higher than those for nonsmokers. Proportionately many more men than women smoke. On the basis of these three factors alone, cigarette smoking is a likely candidate to account for part of the widening mortality gap between the sexes. The importance of cigarette smoking in this regard has in fact been demonstrated by Enterline [1960], Preston [1970a and 1970b], and Mulcahy *et al.* [1970], all of whom used correlation and regression techniques to approach the problem for a number of Western countries with available data on overall per capita cigarette consumption. The contribution of cigarette smoking to excess widowhood in the United States has been estimated by Grannis [1970] and Retherford [1973], who both found it to be substantial.

This chapter attempts to evaluate quantitatively, by methods not used previously, the effect of smoking on the sex mortality differential, as measured by the female-male difference in both life-expectancy and the standardized death rate. Attention is restricted to the United States, because the detailed mortality data (specific for age, sex, and smoking status) required for the analysis are limited to a single United States study, carried out by the American Cancer Society (ACS).

TOBACCO CONSUMPTION TRENDS
IN THE UNITED STATES

Table 13 presents evidence for the dramatic increase in per capita cigarette consumption in the United States in this century. Consumption was low before 1920, more than doubled between 1920 and 1930, and doubled again between 1940 and 1960. The considerable decrease in consumption of pipe, cigar, and chewing tobacco over the same period was outweighed by the increase in cigarette consumption.

Table 13

CONSUMPTION OF TOBACCO PRODUCTS PER PERSON
AGED 15 YEARS AND OVER IN THE UNITED STATES
FOR SELECTED YEARS, 1900-1962

Year	All tobacco, pounds	Ciga-rettes, number	Cigars, number	Pipe tobacco, pounds	Chewing tobacco, pounds	Snuff, pounds
1900	7.42	49	111	1.63	4.10	.32
1910	8.59	138	113	2.58	3.99	.50
1920	8.66	611	117	1.96	3.06	.50
1930	8.88	1,365	72	1.87	1.90	.46
1940	8.91	1,828	56	2.05	1.00	.38
1950	11.59	3,322	50	.94	.78	.36
1960	10.97	3,888	57	.59	.51	.29
1961	11.15	3,986	56	.59	.51	.27
1962	10.85	3,958	55	.56	.50	.26

Source: US, HEW, 1956b, p. 45.

The available evidence indicates that the mortality effects of tobacco smoking stem mainly from cigarettes. The small effects of pipe and cigar smoking are indicated by the much lower smoker-nonsmoker mortality ratios for pipe and cigar smokers than for cigarette smokers. For five major studies reviewed in the Surgeon General's 1964 report, smoker-nonsmoker mortality ratios ranged from 1.44 to 1.83 for cigarette smokers and from .86 to 1.11 for pipe and cigar smokers [US, HEW, 1964b:85]. At first sight, the studies (two of the five) for which the ratios for pipe and cigar smokers were less than one seem to imply that pipe and cigar smoking actually tended to decrease mortality for the persons studied. More detailed examination of the data suggests that these inconsistencies were due to the intrusion of factors unrelated to smoking, because within the pipe and cigar smoking populations, smoker-nonsmoker mortality ratios were in almost all cases higher for those who smoked more [US, HEW, 1964b:86-87]. It appears, then, that the effects of pipe and cigar smoking are adverse, but small in comparison to those of cigarette smoking.

Since pipe and cigar smoking have been almost exclusively confined to males, the steep declines in per capita consumption of pipe and cigar tobacco have undoubtedly operated to decrease slightly the sex mortality differential at the same time that sharp increases in per capita cigarette consumption have tended to widen it greatly. Hence the contribution of all forms of tobacco smoking combined to increases in the sex mortality differential probably underestimates the contribution of cigarette smoking alone.

In February 1955, the Bureau of the Census, on behalf of the National Cancer Institute, collected smoking histories as a supplement to the Current Population Survey. The findings corroborate that proportionally many more men smoke than women. It was found that 68.0 percent of men but only 32.4 percent of women had ever smoked cigarettes. Furthermore, among the nonsmokers, more men than women had previously smoked cigarettes regularly (9.8 compared to 3.1 percent), and among the current regular cigarette smokers, more men than women smoked more than 20 cigarettes a day

(13.6 compared to 2.4 percent) [US, HEW, 1956b:8].

In 1966 Hammond reported even more detailed comparisons of male and female smoking habits, based on the American Cancer Society study. This study generally verified the National Cancer Institute findings, and in addition found that the male smokers inhaled more deeply than the female smokers and that they began smoking at an earlier age [Hammond, 1966:128].

In sum, the above evidence of increasingly important sex differentials in smoking habits supports the hypothesis that smoking trends have played an important role in the evolution of the sex mortality differential (SMD) during this century.

EFFECT OF TOBACCO SMOKING ON THE SMD

In Chapters 3 and 4, it was found that the causes of death most closely linked to smoking—cardiovascular diseases, neoplasms, and respiratory diseases at the older ages—accounted for most of the increase in the sex mortality differential between 1910 and 1965. Causes of death less directly related or unrelated to smoking either had a small positive effect or contributed negatively. The link to smoking, however, was indirect, since other factors, such as diet, exercise, and stress, also affect mortality from these causes, particularly cardiovascular diseases.

In this section we evaluate directly (1) the percentage of the SMD in 1962 that is due to smoking and (2) the percentage of the change in the SMD between 1910 and 1962 that is due to smoking. Each of these two percentages is decomposed into a sum of contributions by age and ICD cause of death.

The 1962 data source is the American Cancer Society study of smoking in relation to the death rates of one million men and women [Hammond, 1966], carried out from 1959 to 1964. Unfortunately the ACS sample was not a probability sample from the United States population, although efforts were made to make it as representative as possible. Non-married persons, hospitalized persons, and the lower socio-economic groups were underrepresented, so that the study population was healthier than the actual United States population [Hammond, 1969:952]. As a result, $_{50}e_{35}$ (life expectancy between ages 35 and 85) was about two years higher and the F-M difference in $_{50}e_{35}$ about .5 year higher in the sample population than in the United States population in 1962. On the other hand, comparison of the ACS sample with the National Cancer Institute 1955 probability sample of the United States population shows close agreement between the two samples in the proportion of persons who never smoked cigarettes regularly in each age-sex category [US, HEW, 1956b: 74-75; Hammond, 1966:174-176]. In the following analysis the ACS study population is considered reasonably representative of the United States population in 1962, but because of sample biases, the results obtained must be viewed as only approximately valid.

Table 14 shows the life expectancy data to be analyzed. Attention is restricted to the 37-86 age range, which corres-

Table 14

FEMALE-MALE DIFFERENCES IN $_{50}e_{37}$ (LIFE EXPECTANCY BETWEEN AGES 37 AND 87), UNITED STATES, 1910, AND AMERICAN CANCER SOCIETY STUDY, 1962

		M	F	F-M
U.S. 1910[a]		29.32	31.20	1.88
ACS study, 1962	Cigarette smokers	35.44	41.33	5.89
	Non-smokers	39.93	42.64	2.71
	Total sample	37.24	42.37	5.13

[a]Values of $_{50}e_{37}$ for the U.S. in 1910 were calculated from life tables for the original Death Registration Area [U.S. Bureau of the Census, 1921].

ponds to the age range of the published data. (The ACS
35-84 age range is interpolated forward two years, to allow
for the fact that mortality rates were originally tabulated
according to age of subjects at the beginning rather than the
middle of the study.)

We consider first the percentage of the F-M difference in
$_{50}e_{37}$ (life expectancy between ages 37 and 87) in 1962 that
is accounted for by all forms of smoking combined. If no one
in the ACS sample had ever smoked, then, if one were to
assume that spurious effects due to the correlation of tobacco
consumption with other mortality-related factors are negligible,
the F-M difference in $_{50}e_{37}$ for the total sample would have
been the same as that for nonsmokers. Table 14 shows that it
would have been 2.71 years instead of 5.13 years, a reduction
of 47.2 percent. We interpret this to mean that tobacco smoking accounts for 47.2 percent of the F-M difference in $_{50}e_{37}$
in the United States in 1962. In reality, of course, spurious
factors are present. For example, there is evidence that job
stress and alcoholism are correlated with cigarette consumption,
although these two factors appear to be of minor significance
[Preston, 1970a and 1970b; see also Chap. 2] . Cigarette consumption differentials by such mortality-related characteristics
as socioeconomic status and psychophysical type may also
explain part of the observed effects of smoking, although there
is no evidence that they play an important role.

The age-ICD cause breakdown of this 47.2 percent effect of
smoking is obtained as follows. If we represent the SMD in the
total sample by SMD_{ts} and that of nonsmokers by SMD_{ns}, then
47.2 percent corresponds to $(SMD_{ts} - SMD_{ns})/SMD_{ts}$. The
numerator of this quantity is decomposed in a manner mathematically identical to that used earlier to decompose the change
in the SMD over time. Each unpercentaged age-cause contribution to $(SMD_{ts} - SMD_{ns})/SMD_{ts}$ is then obtained as $1/SMD_{ts}$ of
the corresponding contribution to $(SMD_{ts} - SMD_{ns})$. When considered in percentaged terms the decompositions of $(SMD_{ts} -$

SMD_{ns}) and $(SMD_{ts} - SMD_{ns})/SMD_{ts}$ are identical.

Of the 47.2 percent smoking effect, the left half of Table 15 shows that 46.8 percent is accounted for by coronary heart disease, acting primarily at ages 47-66. Cerebrovascular lesions contribute almost negligibly. The published data do not allow a more detailed cause breakdown in Table 15, but it appears reasonably certain, as will be argued later, that cancer accounts for most of the "other" contribution. The residuals are small, so that the interpretation of the table is relatively clear.

To estimate the percentage change in the sex mortality differential between 1910 and 1962 attributable to tobacco smoking, we need to make two assumptions. First, that in 1910 per capita consumption was negligible for cigarettes. Second, that although it was relatively high for pipe and cigar tobacco, the effect on mortality generally and on the SMD particularly was trifling. Table 13 and the stated mortality effects of pipe and cigar smoking suggest that these assumptions are not unreasonable, although they by no means square perfectly with reality. As before, we need also to assume that spurious effects due to the correlation of tobacco consumption with other mortality-related factors are inconsequential.

We now reason as follows: If cigarette smoking had remained at a negligible level, the F-M difference in $_{50}e_{37}$ in 1962 would have been about the same as it actually was for sample nonsmokers, namely 2.71 years (Table 14). Hence the 1962 total population-nonsmoker differential in $(_{50}e_{37}^{f} - _{50}e_{37}^{m})$, evaluated from the sample, represents the fraction of the 1910-1962 increase in $(_{50}e_{37}^{f} - _{50}e_{37}^{m})$ that is due to smoking. Since the former differential is 2.42 years and the latter 3.25 years, we conclude that 74.5 percent of the increase in the F-M difference in $_{50}e_{37}$ in the United States between 1910 and 1962 is accounted for by changes in smoking habits.

The age-ICD cause decomposition of this 74.5 percent smoking effect is identical to that given in the left half of Table 15. Let SMD_{ts} and SMD_{ns} represent the sex mortality

Table 15

DECOMPOSITION OF THE EFFECT OF SMOKING ON THE F-M DIFFERENCE IN $_{50}e_{37}$ (LIFE EXPECTANCY BETWEEN AGES 37 AND 87), AMERICAN CANCER SOCIETY STUDY, 1962

Age	Total sample: effect of all forms of smoking combined					Cigarette smokers only: effect of cigarette smoking				
	CHD[a]	CVL	Other	Residual	Total	CHD	CVL	Other	Residual	Total
37-46	8.8	-.0	4.9	.0	13.7	7.9	-.0	5.0	.1	12.9
47-56	15.8	-.2	10.6	.2	26.5	15.0	-.7	9.7	.3	24.3
57-66	14.1	.9	16.6	.5	32.1	11.5	-.3	18.2	.9	30.3
67-76	5.5	.7	11.9	.3	18.5	2.6	-.3	12.1	1.0	15.4
77-86	1.6	-.5	3.0	.0	4.1	1.2	-1.7	5.3	.1	5.0
R	1.0	-.0	1.3	2.8	5.1	1.9	-.0	3.5	6.6	12.0
T	46.8	.8	48.4	3.9	100.0	40.0	-3.0	53.8	9.1	100.0
					(47.2)[b]					(54.0)[c]

[a]CHD is coronary heart disease, and CVL is cerebrovascular lesions.

[b]Percentage of the F-M difference in $_{50}e_{37}$ for the total sample accounted for by smoking.

[c]Percentage of the F-M difference in $_{50}e_{37}$ for cigarette smokers accounted for by cigarette smoking.

differentials for total sample and nonsmokers, as before, and let SMD_{1910} represent the sex mortality differential in the United States in 1910. Then 74.5 percent corresponds to $(SMD_{ts} - SMD_{ns})/(SMD_{ts} - SMD_{1910})$. Since the numerator of this quantity is the same as the numerator of $(SMD_{ts} - SMD_{ns})/SMD_{ts}$, decomposed in the left half of Table 15, the per-centaged decompositions are clearly the same.

Actually, the mortality effects of the decline in per capita consumption of pipe and cigar tobacco cannot be discounted entirely. They undoubtedly acted to narrow the sex mortality differential over this period as the increases in cigarette consumption concomitantly acted to widen it. Hence the figure of 74.5 percent for the effect of all forms of smoking combined on the change in the F-M difference in $_{50}e_{37}$ may actually underestimate the effect of cigarette smoking alone.

THE SMD FOR CIGARETTE SMOKERS

With the ACS data at our disposal, we can evaluate the effect of cigarette smoking alone on the sex mortality differential in the subpopulation of cigarette smokers in 1962. The reasoning parallels that used in the last section to assess the effect of all forms of smoking combined on the sex mortality differential in the total population.

Table 14 shows F-M differences in $_{50}e_{37}$ of 2.71 and 5.89 years for nonsmokers and cigarette smokers respectively. Non-smokers therefore have an F-M difference in $_{50}e_{37}$ that is 54.0 percent less than the corresponding value for cigarette smokers, or, in other words, cigarette smoking accounts for 54.0 percent of the F-M difference in $_{50}e_{37}$ for cigarette smokers. As ex-pected, this value is higher than the 47.2 percent obtained earlier for the effect of all forms of smoking combined on the SMD in the total population, since in this latter case the density of cigarette smokers is less than unity and the effects of cigarette smoking are therefore attenuated.

The 54.0 percent of the F-M difference in $_{50}e_{37}$ among cigarette smokers accounted for by cigarette smoking is decomposed by age and ICD cause of death in the right half of Table 15, which is identical in format to and obtained in the same way as the left half. The coronary heart disease contribution on the right is 40.0 percent, somewhat less than the 46.8 percent on the left, and again it is concentrated mainly at ages 47-66. Contributions from cerebrovascular lesions are mostly negative and close to zero in both decompositions. They are negative because for most age groups, female CVL mortality rates are more aggravated by cigarette smoking than the corresponding male rates; but these CVL mortality differences are small, and not much significance can be attached to them because of the small numbers of CVL deaths involved [Hammond, 1966: App. Table 17].

Although the American Cancer Society has not published detailed age-sex-smoking status-specific mortality data for causes other than coronary heart disease and cerebrovascular lesions, it has published age-standardized death rates for a more detailed list of causes for the age range 47-66 by sex, smoking status (cigarette smokers, nonsmokers), and cause. Values of SDR(47-66) can be analyzed in a manner identical to that leading to the right half of Table 15, except that in this case only a cause breakdown of the smoking effect, rather than an age-cause breakdown, is possible. In Table 16 the M-F difference in SDR(47-66) is 64.9 percent less for nonsmokers than for cigarette smokers, so that, equivalently, cigarette smoking accounts for 64.9 percent of the M-F difference in SDR(47-66) for cigarette smokers. Coronary heart disease contributes 51.8 percent of the effect and cancer 29.0 percent. Together cardiovascular diseases and cancer account for 89.1 percent. The percentage distribution in Table 16 is very similar to that for excess deaths among men with a history of regular cigarette smoking in a study preliminary to the ACS study

[Hammond and Horn, 1958:1307]. It gives a rough idea of what the cause marginals of Table 15 might look like if they were more complete.

The overwhelming importance of CHD in Tables 15 and 16 may at first seem puzzling, since cigarette smoker-nonsmoker mortality ratios (of age-standardized mortality rates) are much higher for lung cancer and the degenerative lung diseases than for CHD. For example, seven prospective studies in the Surgeon General's 1964 report show cigarette smoker-nonsmoker mortality ratios of 10.8, 6.1, and 1.7 for lung cancer, bronchitis and emphysema, and CHD, respectively [US, HEW, 1964b:28]. The explanation of this apparent contradiction hinges on overall mortality rates being very low for lung cancer and the degenerative lung diseases compared to the rate for CHD. The

Table 16

DECOMPOSITION OF THE EFFECT OF CIGARETTE SMOKING ON THE M-F DIFFERENCE IN SDR(47-66) (AGE-STANDARDIZED DEATH RATE FOR AGES 47-66) FOR CIGARETTE SMOKERS, AMERICAN CANCER SOCIETY STUDY, 1962

Coronary heart disease	51.8
Other heart and circulatory	8.3
Lung cancer	14.3
Other cancer	14.7
Violence, accidents, suicide	.6
Other	10.3
Total	100.0
	(64.9)[a]

[a]Among cigarette smokers SDR(47-66) was 1,300 for males, 568 for females, and 732 for the M-F difference. Corresponding figures for nonsmokers were 698, 441, and 257. The value 64.9 represents the percentage of the M-F difference in SDR(47-66) for cigarette smokers accounted for by cigarette smoking.

Source: Computed from data in Hammond [1966:156, 160].

1.7-fold increase in deaths from CHD therefore produces many more excess deaths than either the 10.8-fold increase in deaths from lung cancer or the 6.1-fold increase in deaths from bronchitis and emphysema. It is the excess deaths and not the ratios that are reflected most accurately in the decompositions. A related point was made earlier in Chapter 3 where the decompositions more accurately reflected sex mortality differences than sex mortality ratios.

In sum, that cardiovascular disease and cancer account for most of the increase in the sex mortality differential between 1910 and 1965 appears to be explained primarily by the fact that the effect of smoking on the sex mortality differential is large and felt mainly through these same diseases. Employing a very different measure of excess male mortality and for the most part different data sources, Preston (1970a and 1970b) used correlation and regression techniques to reach essentially the same conclusion for a cross section of Western countries. Given the contrast in approach to the problem between the two studies, the parallel findings can be regarded as complementary.

7 Marital Status and the Sex Mortality Differential

MARITAL STATUS AND MORTALITY BY AGE AND CAUSE

Much of the United States literature on mortality by marital status has been based on two special reports for 1940 and 1949-1951 [US, HEW, PHS, 1943, 1956a]. A third report for 1959-1961 appeared more recently [US, HEW, PHS, 1970]. Studies stemming from these reports have focused primarily on nonmarried-married mortality differentials for each sex separately. Variations in sex mortality differentials by marital status have received little direct attention.

Dublin *et al.* [1949] used the 1940 data to compute non-married/married (NM/M) mortality ratios of age-specific rates for the single, widowed, and divorced. They noted that non-married groups had higher mortality than the married and that this marital status mortality differential was more marked for males than for females. They also sought to determine the causes of death most responsible for excess nonmarried mortality, and to this end examined NM/M mortality ratios of age-standardized mortality rates for each cause. The two out-standing causes were tuberculosis and syphilis. Influenza and pneumonia were also important, as were cirrhosis of the liver, suicide, accidents, and homicide. Other causes were less important, although almost all showed ratios considerably greater than one.

The 1949-1951 data show a rather similar pattern. However, Shurtleff [1956] also singled out diseases of the heart for comment, in spite of their relatively low NM/M mortality ratio, because they accounted in 1949-1951 for such a high proportion of total deaths, regardless of marital status. The 1959-1961 report, which methodologically relies less on NM/M ratios than the earlier reports, shows a decline in the importance of tuberculosis and syphilis (data for syphilis are not even presented) and a rise in the importance of neoplasms, circulatory diseases, and diabetes [US, HEW, PHS, 1970]. At all three dates, 1940, 1949-1951, and 1959-1961, NM/M mortality ratios were usually highest for divorced persons, followed by those for widowed and single persons, the pattern being more pronounced for males than for females.

Sheps [1961] investigated the possibility that the marital status mortality differentials observed in the 1949-1951 data were due in part to systematic biases in the data. The base for each mortality rate in the 1949-1951 report was an estimate of the 1950 population derived from a 19.95 percent sample of the population. Noting some irregularities in the procedure used by the Census Bureau to obtain this sample, Sheps compared it to the complete 1950 census count of the population by marital status. The estimated totals from the sample for the three categories, single, married, and widowed or divorced for each sex separately, were found in every case to be within 2 percent of the corresponding figures from the complete census count. Males were slightly underestimated in the sample, relative to the complete count, and females slightly overestimated, except for single persons, who were underestimated for both sexes. The discrepancies were not large enough to affect either mortality rates or SMDs significantly.

Of course, it is possible that similar biases were at work in both sample and complete census counts, in which case Sheps' comparison is not very illuminating. For example, misstatements about marital status occur mostly among individuals living alone, and such misstatements no doubt occurred in both the sample and the complete census counts [Shurtleff,

1956:655] . Jacobson [1959:5ff.] has estimated that the undercount of divorced persons in the 1950 census was 20 percent for males and 21 percent for females and that the undercount for earlier censuses was probably even higher. Some of the undercount stems from misreporting. Many divorced persons are no doubt hesitant to reveal their status to the enumerator. Also, particularly in the case of divorced males, who ordinarily do not have custody of children and who frequently are not at home when the enumerator comes by, a divorced person is likely to be reported to the enumerator as single by neighbors who are unaware of his true status. Mortality rates by marital status can be biased both by the census information and the death data used. Jacobson [1959:5] opined that the relative errors for divorced persons are smallest on death certificates and largest on census schedules. He concluded that at least in population counts of divorced persons, the magnitude of distortion appears so large that related statistics should be used with extreme caution.

Kraus and Lilienfeld [1959:211], in their study of the especially high mortality of the young widowed group (as measured by widowed/married mortality ratios at ages 20-34), based on the 1949-1951 data, also examined the possibility that misclassification might be partly responsible. They noted that if census errors were solely responsible, one would expect identical cause-specific NM/M ratios for the various causes of death for a given age-sex-marital status group, whereas in fact NM/M mortality ratios varied a great deal by cause. They made the same point about misstatements of marital status on death certificates.

Having concluded that misclassification was not extensive enough to explain very much of the relative excess mortality of the young widowed group, Kraus and Lilienfeld suggested several alternative hypotheses. The first of these they called the selection hypothesis.

This explanation assumes that the subsequent mortality rate of all those who became widowed is no different than for those of the same age who remained married. However, it hypothesized that those who became widowed and were in good health tended to remarry and return themselves to the married population, while the ill who became widowed tended to remain widowed and be classified as such in both the census and on the death certificates if death occurred. Thus the group remaining widowed would have higher mortality rates than the married because they tended to be "selected" in terms of ill health.

By means of a hypothetical example, Kraus and Lilienfeld found that even when selection is assumed strong (for persons classified as widowed in 1949, deaths over the three years 1949 to 1951 were assumed to have occurred only to those who did not remarry over the same period), its effect is still small compared to the observed excess mortality of the young widowed group.

The selective effects of remarriage could be eliminated by restricting comparisons to the single and ever-married [Zalokar, 1960], but at the cost of obscuring possible differences between the causal effects of marriage widowhood, and divorce on mortality. Zalokar compared mortality for single and ever-married women by means of single/ever-married mortality ratios and found young single women to be particularly disadvantaged. The extent to which selective marriage on the basis of health accounts for this pattern is unclear.

Selective marriage or remarriage on the basis of health also shapes the relation of marital status to the SMD. Because of excess male mortality, there is at the older ages, where sex ratios are lopsidedly feminine, a relative shortage of males. This makes it easier for a man in poor health to retain or find a mate than for a woman in a similar state of poor health. No doubt in part because of this selective factor, nonmarried males at the older ages tend to be in poorer health relative to nonmarried females than married males are relative to married females, producing wider SMDs at the older ages for the nonmarried than for the married.

Kraus and Lilienfeld advanced a second hypothesis to explain the relative excess mortality in the young widowed population—the "mutual choice of poor-risk mates." According to this theory, which also construes a type of selection, individuals with given types of disabilities tend to marry persons similarly disabled. It gains some support from a study by Ciocco [1940a], who analyzed causes of death among a sample of 2,571 white married couples who died in Washington County, Maryland, from 1898 to 1938. He found a tendency for spouses to die from the same cause, not only from infectious diseases but also, to a lesser extent, from heart disease and cancer as well. The association between husband and wife mortality from infectious diseases can obviously be explained by the spread of infection in the family environment, but for heart disease and cancer, Ciocco felt that some kind of conscious or unconscious marital selection must also be considered as a possible explanation. Not all studies verify Ciocco's implied finding of excess mortality from heart disease among the widowed, but the conflicting evidence is mostly from studies based on small samples, not national coverage [Marks, 1967: 90-91].

Ciocco's findings are consistent not only with the mutual choice of poor-risk mates hypothesis, but also with what Kraus and Lilienfeld have termed the "joint unfavorable environment" hypothesis (yet another type of selection). They theorize that spouses share common unfavorable environmental factors which lead to the death of the first spouse and result in excessive risk to the survivor. Ciocco's finding of associated husband-wife mortality from infectious diseases is particularly amenable to this interpretation, but because of such factors as diet and smoking habits, mortality from heart disease and cancer must also be considered. Sheps [1961:550] has pointed out a particularly obvious instance where the joint unfavorable environment interpretation applies, namely the relative excess in widowed mortality from motor vehicle accidents.

> It is likely that when both partners to a marriage are fatally injured in the same accident the earlier death is counted as married and the second as widowed. Since both were in the married population, this could artifically tend to decrease the married mortality rate and increase the widowed mortality rate.

She also observed that the same pattern might be expected in other types of deaths occurring close together, such as deaths from acute infectious diseases. The more frequent occurrence of widowhood in the lower socioeconomic groups, which in general experience higher mortality than do the upper strata, also constitutes evidence in support of the joint unfavorable environment hypothesis.

Young *et al.* [1963] studied a cohort of 4,486 widowers of 55 years and over whose wives died in 1957. The data were obtained from the General Register Office of England and Wales. The investigators followed this cohort for five years, calculating mortality rates for the first six months and second six months of duration, and for each year of duration thereafter. They found that the ratio of widowed to married rates was highest within the first six months of widowhood. They concluded that the sudden short-run increase in widowed mortality found in their data was consistent with any one of several hypotheses. These are homogamy (same as mutual choice of poor-risk mates), common infection, joint unfavorable environment, and loss of care. The first three we have already discussed. The authors explain about the fourth:

> Widowers may become malnourished when they no longer have wives to look after them. They may also go to their doctor less and take their medicine less diligently when they no longer have someone to prod them—although the reverse is also possible. Widowers may consult their doctors more often and expose themselves to more infections and other hazards as a consequence. Having to adapt to a changed social role as a result of losing a spouse may itself impair resistance to disease.

Cox and Ford [1964] conducted a similar study of 60,000

widows, based on 1933 data from the Decennial Review of
the National Contributory Pensions System. The women were
followed over a five-year period. The ratio of actual to expected deaths for each of the five years after inception of
widowhood, calculated by dividing the mortality rate for a
given year by that for all five years combined, showed mortality
to be greatest during the second year of widowhood. Why
excess mortality peaked in the second instead of the first year
of widowhood is not entirely clear. The authors suggest that
it may have been because widows who died shortly after their
husbands may not yet have applied for pensions.

Kraus and Lilienfeld [1959:214] have remarked that the
relative excess of mortality among the young widowed may
be due in part to the event and new conditions of widowhood
itself. This "effects of widowhood" hypothesis, which is
somewhat similar to Young *et al.*'s loss of care hypothesis,
includes the effects of the grief, the new worries and responsi-
bilities, alterations in the diet, work regimen, and recreational
life, and the frequently reduced economic condition. Most of
these effects apply to divorced persons as well. On the other
side of the coin, Sheps [1961:547] has hypothesized a real
protective effect associated with marriage. Shurtleff [1956:659]
has suggested that married family life may be conducive to
greater regularity in the pattern of eating, sleeping, working,
and playing, relative to the corresponding pattern for nonmarried persons. Married persons may have stronger motivation
to guard their health for the sake of partners and dependents.
The single person may work in relatively more hazardous jobs
and indulge more freely in his living habits. Moreover, the
stabilizing and moderating influences of family life may be
greater for males than for females, because society and perhaps
temperament limit the behavior pattern of the unmarried man
less than that of the unmarried woman.

This latter factor bears directly on the relation of marital
status to the SMD. In addition, women may be better con-

ditioned to cope with the nonmarried state than are men. A man's life, aside from his immediate family, tends to revolve around his work, which is characterized by relatively competitive and impersonal relationships. Women, on the other hand, tend to be more embedded in a web of personal relationships and friendships that extend beyond the nuclear family. It can therefore be argued that the nonmarried state possibly involves less in the way of painful personal and emotional adjustments or readjustments for women than for men and that this is perhaps partly responsible for the greater mortality impact of the nonmarried state on men than on women. This view is supported by studies of psychological well-being and mental illness, which also show marital status differentials much greater for men than for women [Gove, 1973].

We can subsume the presumed effects of all the above marital status-related factors under the heading, the "effects of marital status" hypothesis, which includes Young et al.'s loss of care, Kraus and Lilienfeld's effects of widowhood, and Sheps' and Shurtleff's protective effect associated with marriage.

In sum, we have examined three principal hypotheses about why nonmarried exceeds married mortality. These involve misclassification (misreporting and underenumeration), selection (selective marriage or remarriage on the basis of health, mutual choice of poor-risk mates, joint unfavorable environment), and effects of marital status. The order of importance of these hypotheses, all of which have some basis in fact, is not clear, although for the young widowed group at least, misclassification and selective remarriage on the basis of health appear relatively unimportant.

THE SMD AND MARITAL STATUS

With mortality rates by marital status, sex, age, and ICD

cause, we can analyze the relation between marital status and the SMD in a manner mathematically similar to that used to analyze the relation of smoking to the SMD. For marital status, however, the results are ambiguous, because it is unclear how much of the variation in the SMD by marital status is from causal effects of marital status on mortality and how much to misclassification and selection.

Detailed classifications of mortality by marital status, sex, age, and cause are available for only a few countries at one or two dates. Treated here are the United States in 1950 (1949-1951), France in 1951, and West Germany in 1961, countries for which data were readily available when this research was done. For the United States and France, the original data were already grouped somewhat by cause, so that it was unfortunately not possible to use the same cause breakdown from Chapters 3 and 4. The cause categories used in this chapter are as follows:

TB	Tuberculosis
SYPH	Syphilis
NEO	Neoplasms
DIAB	Diabetes
C-R	Cardiovascular-renal
RESP	Respiratory
DIG	Digestive
MAT	Maternal mortality
ACC	Accidents, poisonings, violence, suicide
OTH	All other causes

In the French data, maternal deaths by marital status were not given and were therefore included in the "other" category for that country. Also, for the United States and France, the age groups differed somewhat from the conventional abridged life table age groups, so the original data were interpolated where necessary to give this conventional grouping (see Appendix A).

The measure of mortality is the expectation of life at age 20, denoted e_{20}. Values of this measure by country, sex, and marital status are shown in Table 17. SMDs for the single, widowed, and divorced are vastly greater than those for the married, with the puzzling exception of the divorced in France, whose SMD is almost as low as that of the married. In the United States the divorced have the highest SMD of any of the three nonmarried groups. In France and Germany the widowed have the highest. In Germany general mortality as is measured by e_{20} is highest for the divorced and the SMD highest for the widowed, whereas in France both are highest for the widowed. It is possible that the excessively high mortality and SMD for divorced persons in the United States, compared to France and Germany, is due to more extensive undernumeration and misreporting of divorced persons than in the other two countries. Earlier it was noted that these kinds of errors have been large in United States census counts.

If we lump the single, widowed, and divorced together and deal only with the married, nonmarried, and total populations, the relative order of sizes of SMDs by marital status is fairly similar for all three countries. France is again a partial exception, where even for married persons the SMD is slightly greater than that for the total population. At first sight, it might seem impossible that the SMD for the total population could be less than the SMDs of each of the marital status subgroups that together comprise the total population. This can nevertheless occur because of the widely differing age-sex distributions within each marital status.

Table 18 shows the ICD cause contributions to the non-married-married differential in $(e_{20}^f - e_{20}^m)$ for each nonmarried category in each of the three countries. The cause categories that stand out are cardiovascular-renal diseases, accidents, tuberculosis, and "other." (Again, the divorced in France depart markedly from the pattern.) The large accidents and tuberculosis contributions square well with findings from the earlier literature, but the large cardiovascular-renal contribu-

Table 17

SEX DIFFERENTIALS IN e_{20} BY MARITAL STATUS, UNITED STATES 1949-1951, FRANCE 1951, AND WEST GERMANY 1961

	United States			France			Germany		
	M	F	F-M	M	F	F-M	M	F	F-M
S[a]	44.12	53.06	8.94	44.50	52.02	7.52	47.54	54.67	7.13
M	50.93	55.42	4.49	50.26	55.29	5.03	51.54	56.15	4.61
W	41.20	49.84	8.64	41.51	51.12	9.62	41.94	54.30	12.36
D	40.60	50.27	9.67	47.68	53.12	5.44	45.23	53.22	7.99
NM	43.72	51.82	8.10	44.68	52.05	7.37	46.97	54.75	7.78
T	49.00	53.90	4.90	48.68	53.67	4.98	50.54	55.32	4.78

[a]S = single, M = married, W = widowed, D = divorced, NM = nonmarried (S+W+D), T = total.

Table 18

CAUSE CONTRIBUTIONS TO THE NONMARRIED-MARRIED DIFFERENCE IN $(e^f_{20} - e^m_{20})$ FOR EACH NONMARRIED CATEGORY, UNITED STATES 1949-1951, FRANCE 1951, AND GERMANY 1961

		TB[a]	SYPH	NEO	DIAB	C-R	RESP	DIG	MAT	ACC	OTH	Residual	TOTAL
US	S	10.5	1.5	-.6	3.6	27.9	3.3	6.2	1.7	13.1	14.4	18.4	100.0 (4.45)
	W	21.6	2.7	-.1	.0	21.2	5.8	5.7	-.3	31.7	36.6	-25.0	100.0 (4.14)
	D	17.5	3.1	.7	1.6	30.4	6.4	10.8	.8	33.1	31.2	-35.8	100.0 (5.18)
	NM	18.7	2.5	2.8	1.7	27.1	6.7	9.8	1.9	24.1	26.6	-21.8	100.0 (3.61)
FR	S	10.9	.6	1.2	1.9	15.3	.7	6.6	—	27.9	18.6	16.2	100.0 (2.49)
	W	26.5	-.6	8.0	2.9	20.5	4.9	2.5	—	33.6	21.6	-19.8	100.0 (4.58)
	D	146.2	-1.1	-75.7	12.4	-50.5	-8.0	-8.8	—	93.7	-20.5	12.3	100.0 (0.41)
	NM	22.9	.6	1.0	.5	15.6	2.5	6.9	—	34.7	30.2	-15.0	100.0 (2.34)
GE	S	5.8	.5	-4.9	3.2	23.5	1.8	4.9	4.3	29.2	22.6	9.0	100.0 (2.52)
	W	1.8	-.0	7.5	.5	16.4	2.2	2.7	1.6	71.0	7.0	-10.7	100.0 (7.75)
	D	11.3	1.4	2.6	1.0	10.4	8.0	9.0	1.2	53.3	18.9	-17.1	100.0 (3.38)
	NM	8.1	.6	6.7	1.3	23.1	4.8	6.3	3.3	33.4	23.5	-11.1	100.0 (3.17)

[a]Cause categories in this chapter differ from those used in Chapters 3 and 4. See text for discussion.

tions and the small syphilis and respiratory contributions do not. The reason for the discrepancy is that nonmarried/married mortality ratios, on which most of the earlier literature is based, can be large when nonmarried-married mortality differences are small, as shown in Table 19. A related point was made in Chapter 6, which discussed the apparent discrepancy between smoker/nonsmoker mortality ratios and smoker-nonsmoker mortality differences in coronary heart disease, and in Chapter 3, which noted that decompositions of the SMD and changes in it more accurately reflected sex mortality differences than sex mortality ratios of age-cause-specific rates. Cause-specific sex mortality differences and sex mortality ratios by marital status show a similar contrast, as illustrated in Table 20. NM/M or M/F mortality ratios for a particular subgroup, such as young widowed persons, or a particular cause, such as syphilis, may be useful for assessing the strength of the impact of marital status or sex differences on mortality for that same subgroup or cause but not necessarily for larger aggregates, since the subgroup or cause in question may produce only a minute fraction of total deaths. As with findings from preceding studies, Tables 18 to 20 are not especially helpful for distinguishing causal from selection effects, nor for ranking in order of importance the various hypotheses put forth to explain the statistical relationships between marital status and mortality and the SMD.

In view of the large effects of cigarette smoking on the SMD, could it be that marital status differentials in smoking explain away part of the apparent effect of marital status on the SMD? The Surgeon General's Report (US, HEW, PHS, 1964b:364) says: "Smoking (of any kind) is most prevalent among the divorced and widowed and least among those who have never been married, except that among persons over 45, never-marrieds are as likely to be smokers as the married." It thus seems that smoking does account for part of the marital status effect, but it is difficult to say how much without more

Table 19

NONMARRIED-MARRIED MORTALITY DIFFERENCES AND NONMARRIED/MARRIED
MORTALITY RATIOS OF SDR(20+)[a] BY SEX AND CAUSE, UNITED STATES
1949-1951, FRANCE 1951, AND GERMANY 1961

		TB	SYPH	NEO	DIAB	C-R	RESP	DIG	MAT	ACC	OTH	TOTAL
US	M D[b]	.82	.11	.62	.07	3.09	.42	.40	.00	.89	1.49	7.91
	R	3.85	2.32	1.30	1.38	1.40	2.29	2.20	—	2.09	1.90	1.59
	F D	.19	.02	.38	.01	1.39	.14	.06	-.03	.15	.45	2.77
	R	2.19	1.72	1.20	1.03	1.26	1.61	1.36	.42	1.42	1.43	1.29
FR	M D	.88	.02	.04	-.00	1.58	.53	.22	.00	1.01	3.11	7.39
	R	2.02	1.18	1.01	.98	1.24	1.51	1.34	—	1.89	1.54	1.38
	F D	.29	-.00	-.08	-.04	.46	.31	.02	—	.18	1.45	2.58
	R	1.75	.98	.97	.81	1.10	1.46	1.05	—	1.46	1.39	1.20
GE	M D	.33	.02	.30	.04	1.40	.30	.22	.00	1.18	1.67	5.46
	R	2.09	2.44	1.08	1.27	1.21	1.43	1.38	—	2.04	1.49	1.33
	F D	.06	.01	.01	-.01	.25	.09	.00	-.05	.22	.52	1.10
	R	1.82	1.99	1.00	.95	1.05	1.23	1.02	.26	1.44	1.22	1.10

[a]SDR(20+) denotes the age-standardized death rate for ages 20 and over. The standard differs for each country, being the age distribuiton for all sexes and marital statuses combined for the country and date in question.

[b]D = difference, R = ratio.

Table 20

MALE-FEMALE MORTALITY DIFFERENCES AND MALE/FEMALE MORTALITY RATIOS OF SDR(20+) BY CAUSE AND MARITAL STATUS, UNITED STATES 1949-1951, FRANCE 1951, AND GERMANY 1961

		TB	SYPH	NEO	DIAB	C-R	RESP	DIG	MAT	ACC	OTH	TOTAL
US	D[a] M	.12	.05	.17	-.12	2.50	.10	.15	-.06	.47	.61	3.99
	D[a] NM	.75	.15	.40	-.06	4.20	.38	.48	-.02	1.21	1.64	9.14
	R M	1.76	2.80	1.09	.61	1.48	1.41	1.83	.00	2.32	1.58	1.42
	R NM	3.10	3.78	1.18	.81	1.63	2.01	2.98	.00	3.42	2.09	1.74
FR	D M	.47	.04	.85	-.06	1.83	.39	.27	—	.75	2.09	6.63
	D NM	1.06	.06	.97	-.03	2.96	.62	.47	—	1.58	3.75	11.45
	R M	2.22	1.95	1.34	.68	1.39	1.58	1.73	—	2.93	1.57	1.51
	R NM	2.57	2.36	1.40	.82	1.57	1.63	2.22	—	3.78	1.73	1.74
GE	D M	.23	.01	.86	-.07	1.79	.33	.34	-.06	.65	1.03	5.12
	D NM	.49	.03	1.15	-.02	2.95	.54	.56	-.02	1.61	2.18	9.49
	R M	4.17	2.37	1.32	.67	1.36	1.89	2.43	.00	2.32	1.44	1.45
	R NM	4.80	2.80	1.42	.89	1.57	2.19	3.29	.00	3.27	1.76	1.76

[a]D = difference, R = ratio, M = married, NM = nonmarried.

detailed data. Since single persons also have much higher mortality than married persons, yet smoke less, it seems that factors other than smoking must also be important.

What would be the effect of universal marriage on the SMD? If everyone aged 20 and over had been currently married (physically impossible because of unequal numbers of males and females and the lag time between divorce or widowhood and remarriage) and if the relationship between marital status and mortality were completely causal (which it is not), the F-M difference in e_{20} would have been 8.4 percent lower in the United States in 1949-1951, 1.0 percent higher in France in 1951, and 3.6 percent lower in Germany in 1961 than it actually was (calculated from Table 17). For societies as wholes the potential beneficial effect of universal marriage on the SMD is thus small. The apparent discrepancy between the small societal effect of universal marriage and the large individual effects of individual marriage occurs because most persons are already married.

We can also examine the effect on the SMD of the changing distribution of the population by marital status, again assuming strict causality. In the United States in 1949-1951 the F-M difference in e_{20} would have been about 12 percent higher than it actually was if marital structure had remained unchanged from what it was in 1910.[1] The trend toward lower age at marriage and higher proportions married

---

[1] Twelve percent is very approximate. It is based on calculations which reconstitute the overall value of e_{20} for each sex as a weighted sum of e_{20} for each marital status, where the weights are the proportions of that sex in each marital status [calculated from data in U.S. Bureau of the Census, 1960b:15]. Such a procedure, necessary because of inadequate age breakdowns of the population in each marital status in 1910, produces overall values of e_{20} that were found to err by as much as 0.4 year. Ideally the weighting procedure should have been applied to the underlying age-marital status-specific death rates instead of e_{20}.

at all ages was more pronounced for males than for females, so that trends in marital structure acted to brake somewhat the increase in the overall SMD.

Because of misclassification and selection, the actual causal effects of marital status on the SMD, potential or real, are undoubtedly even smaller than the above figures indicate. Despite large variations in the SMD by marital status, changes in marital structure appear to have had little impact on the trend of the SMD in this century.

8 Summary

Sex mortality differentials (SMDs) in the West have increased markedly in the twentieth century. Some important social costs of this trend, conferring social as well as scientific significance to its analysis, are lopsidedly feminine sex ratios at the older ages, related high incidence of widowhood, inflated rates of paternal orphanhood, and economic costs from excess male mortality at ages of maximum earning power.

A large number of studies on both animals and human beings show almost universal inferior male longevity in the animal kingdom. SMDs are therefore related to biological sex differences, but the genetic code varies too slowly for them to have contributed significantly to the sharp increases in human SMDs in this century. Changes in the environment must therefore have been responsible.

Analysis of environmental influences requires distinguishing two levels of causes of death. The first is the immediate medical causes, classified according to the International Classification of Diseases (ICD). The second refers to more external factors, such as smoking, the effects of which cut across and are felt through the ICD causes. The external factors usually mentioned as importantly influencing changes in the SMD are working conditions, health technology, smoking, diet, body weight in relation to height, exercise, and stress.

Working conditions were poor during the last century and early years of this century, and the range of employment available to women restricted. Falling occupational risks have therefore benefited men more than women and have tended

to narrow the SMD. Major respects in which the health technology variable has worked to raise the SMD are the decline in
maternal mortality and the improved detection and treatment
of cancer of the female reproductive organs. Cigarette smoking
is an obvious candidate to account for part of the increase in
the SMD. It is harmful to health, per capita consumption has
risen dramatically since the beginning of the century, and
more men smoke than women.

   Diet, body weight in relation to height, exercise, and stress
are thought to affect the SMD primarily by raising male mortality from coronary heart disease (CHD) relative to female
mortality from this cause. Previous studies of such effects are,
however, inconclusive. Saturated fat intake is positively associated with CHD, but in the United States at least, per
capita intake of saturated fats appears to have changed little
since the beginning of the century. Body weight in relation
to height has a significant effect on mortality only when persons
are overweight by fifty pounds or more. With the emergence of
the slim figure fashion for women, men have gained faster
than women in average weight, but the proportion of the population that is excessively overweight is so small that changes in
it cannot have had much effect on the average SMD for the
entire population. Endurance exercise also reduces CHD
mortality, the primary mechanism appearing to be auxiliary
vascularization of the heart muscle, which increases the
likelihood of recovery from interruptions in the arterial blood
supply to the heart. With urbanization, men on average have
probably experienced more reduction in exercise than women.
However, most farm labor is probably not vigorous enough to
stimulate much auxiliary vascularization. On the whole it seems
likely that the exercise contribution to increases in the SMD is
comparatively small. Psychological stress elevates serum
cholesterol levels and accelerates atherogenesis, but since there
have been no marked fluctuations in CHD mortality during
depressions and wars (World War II brought *declines* in CHD

mortality in occupied countries), this effect is probably not very large. Moreover, the evidence is far from clear that average levels of stress have risen in this century and that men have been more affected than women. The contribution of changing levels of stress to increases in the SMD is therefore probably also small.

Much can be learned from a simple examination of trends in SMDs in age-specific death rates. Male-female differences in age-specific rates have declined sharply below age five, remained fairly static at ages 5-49, and increased sharply above age 50. The trend below five has stemmed largely from declines to near-zero levels in infectious and parasitic mortality for both sexes, suggesting that these causes have tended to reduce the overall SMD, as measured, for example, by the female-male difference in life expectancy. The static pattern between five and fifty suggests that the decline of maternal mortality and the rise of male mortality from motor vehicle accidents have been largely offset by the decline in male mortality from industrial accidents. The trend above fifty suggests the importance of cardiovascular-renal diseases and cancer, since they account for most deaths at the older ages.

Decomposition of the change in the SMD into a sum of age-ICD cause contributions verifies most of these inferences for the United States, England and Wales, and New Zealand between 1910 and 1965. Infectious-parasitic contributions were mostly negative, though not to the extent expected. Positive maternal mortality contributions in the reproductive ages were largely offset by net negative contributions from accidents. Cardiovascular-renal and cancer contributions, concentrated at ages above 40, accounted for most of the increases in SMDs in these countries.

Finer examination of maternal mortality contributions reveals that fertility changes, as far as they affect maternal mortality, have had little impact on changes in SMDs during the past one hundred years. Most of the change in maternal mortality, defined as maternal deaths/woman, has occurred because of changes in maternal mortality, defined as maternal deaths/birth. The impact of fertility change has been even smaller on female longevity than on the SMD.

A detailed analysis of the impact of tobacco smoking trends on the SMD is possible only for the United States, based on American Cancer Society mortality data specific for sex, age, smoking status, and ICD cause of death. Analysis shows that smoking accounted for about 47 percent of the female-male difference in $_{50}e_{37}$ (life expectancy between 37 and 87, the age range of the ACS data) in 1962, and about 75 percent of the increase in the female-male difference in $_{50}e_{37}$ between 1910 and 1962. When these percentage effects of smoking are decomposed each into a sum of contributions by age and ICD cause of death, cardiovascular diseases and cancer at the older ages are found to account for most of the observed effects, consistent with findings from the earlier age-ICD cause analysis. Spurious effects due to the correlation of smoking with other mortality-related factors appear to be small compared to the causal effects of smoking itself.

Variation in SMDs by marital status is very large, the SMD for married persons being low and that for single, widowed, and divorced persons much higher, often by a factor of two or three. Several hypotheses have been put forth to explain this variation. Part of it is probably due to a causal protective effect of marriage. Married life appears conducive to greater regularity in patterns of living and stronger motivation to safeguard health for the sake of partners and dependents. These effects are probably greater for men than for women, since society and perhaps temperament limit the behavior of the unmarried man less than that of the unmarried woman. Moreover, women may be better able to cope with the non-married state than men, since most of them are more embedded in a web of noncompetitive personal relationships and friendships that extend beyond the nuclear family and act to cushion emotional adjustments or readjustments to the non-married state. Noncausal hypotheses involve misclassification of nonmarried persons in census counts, which spuriously increases their mortality rates, and various types of selection, such as selective marriage or remarriage on the basis of health, mutual choice of poor-risk mates, and joint unfavorable environment. ICD causes contributing substantially to nonmarried-married differences in the SMD are cardiovascular-renal diseases, accidents, and tuberculosis, but this pattern offers no firm basis on which to rank the above hypotheses in order of importance.

Even if the observed relationship between marital status and the SMD were completely causal in nature, the effect of universal marriage on the overall SMD would not be large. For example, universal marriage would have meant a female-male difference in e_{20} (life expectancy at age 20) 8.4 percent lower in the United States in 1949-1951, 1.0 percent higher in France in 1951, and 3.6 percent lower in West Germany in 1961. The effect is small because most persons are already married. Under the same assumption of causality, the changing distribution of population by marital status cannot have had much effect on the SMD either. In the United States in 1949-1951 the female-male difference in e_{20} would have been about 12 percent higher had marital structure remained unchanged since 1910. The trend toward lower age at marriage and higher proportions married at all ages was more pronounced for males than for females, so that trends in marital structure acted to brake somewhat the increase in the overall SMD. Because of misclassification and selection, the actual causal effects of marital status on the SMD are undoubtedly even smaller than the above figures indicate.

Of all the factors considered, the contribution of changing smoking patterns to increases in the SMD appears by far the most important.

Appendix A   Data Sources

SOURCES OF AND ADJUSTMENTS TO DATA FOR THE AGE-CAUSE ANALYSIS OF CHAPTERS 3 AND 4

The four dates for which data were collected were 1910, 1930, 1950, and 1965. Some of the necessary 1910 data were lacking for England and Wales and New Zealand, so that 1911 data were used exclusively for these two countries.

For the United States in 1910 death and population data by age and sex for the death registration area were obtained from US Bureau of the Census [1921:428-429]. Corresponding data for 1930, 1950, and 1965 were obtained from Keyfitz and Flieger [1968:145, 170, 176].

For England and Wales in 1911 death and population data by age and sex were obtained from Keyfitz and Flieger [1968: 526]. For 1930, 1950, and 1965 the home population by age and sex was obtained from Great Britain, Registrar-General [1932: Text, p. 99; 1952: Tables, Part 1, Medical, p. 2; 1967: Part 2, p. 4]. Deaths by age and sex for these three dates were obtained from the age-sex marginals of the cause of death data, discussed below.

The New Zealand data are exclusive of Maoris. The New Zealand 1911 midyear population by age and sex was obtained by linearly interpolating the April 2, 1911, and October 15, 1916, census age distributions. The 1930 midyear population by sex in 5-year age groups was obtained from New Zealand, Census and Statistics Office [1931b:27]. The 0-5 age group was separated into conventional 0 and 1-4 age groups using the proportions in these two age groups in the census of April 1, 1931. The 1950 midyear population by age and sex was obtained by linearly interpolating the September 25, 1945, and April 17, 1951, census age distributions. The 1965 midyear population by age and sex was obtained from New Zealand, Dept. of Health [1965: Part 1, p. 1]. The 0-5 age group was separated into 0 and 1-4 age groups using proportions in these two age groups in the census of March 22, 1966. Deaths by age and sex for all four dates were obtained from the age-sex marginals of the cause of death data, discussed below.

For the United States, deaths by age, sex, and cause for the registration areas in 1910 and 1930 were obtained from US Bureau of the Census [1910:348ff; 1930:230ff]. The 1950 data were taken from US, HEW, PHS [1950: vol. 3, pp. 76ff, and vol. 2, pp. 410, 412]. The 1965 data were taken from US, HEW, PHS [1965a, vol. 2, Part A, pp. 1-100ff, 2-40, 2-42].

For England and Wales the cause-of-death data for 1911 were obtained from Great Britain, House of Commons [1913:194ff] and for 1930, 1950, and 1965 from Great Britain, Registrar-General [1932: Tables, Part 1, Medical, pp. 138ff; 1952: Tables, Part 1, Medical, pp. 134ff; 1967: Part 1, pp. 104ff].

For England and Wales in 1930, deaths by cause were given in conventional abridged life table age groups only up to age 80. Deaths by sex and cause in the 80+ age group were inter-polated into 80-84 and 85+ by assuming that sex-cause-specific ratios of mortality rates for these latter two age groups were the same as for New Zealand in 1930.

For New Zealand deaths by age, sex, and cause for 1911 were obtained from New Zealand, Government Statistician [1912: vol. 1, pp. 319ff]. The sources for 1930, 1950, and 1965 were New Zealand, Census and Statistics Office [1931a:68ff] and New Zealand, Dept. of Health [1953:10ff; 1965: Part 1, pp. 16ff, 42ff].

Deaths by age, sex, and cause were converted into age-sex-cause-specific mortality rates as follows. For each sex, overall age-specific mortality rates, M_x, were obtained from the overall death and population data. A set of constants k_x was defined by the relation $M_x = k_x \Sigma_i D_{xi}$. Where the D_{xi} add up to D_x in the numerator of $M_x = D_x/P_x$, k_x is of course equal to $1/P_x$. But this is not true for the United States in 1910 and 1930, where some of the death data pertain just to the registration area. With the k_x calculated, the age-sex-cause-specific rates were obtained as $M_{xi} = k_x D_{xi}$.

SOURCES OF AND ADJUSTMENTS TO DATA FOR THE FERTILITY ANALYSIS OF CHAPTER 5

In Chapter 5 both births and maternal deaths under age 15 were included in the 15-19 age group, and those over age 45 in the 40-44 age group. In some cases this had already been done in the published birth data. Hence the total Maternal (deaths/ woman) contributions in Chapter 5 do not always precisely match those in Chapters 3 and 4.

For the United States 1917 was the first year that birth data were available by age of mother [US, HEW, PHS, 1960]. Age-specific fertility rates for 1910 were obtained by adjusting the 1917 age-specific rates using the ratio of the 1910 to the 1917 value of the birth rate for all women 15-44, obtained from US Bureau of the Census [1960b:23]. Births by age of mother for 1930, 1950, and 1965 were taken from Keyfitz and Flieger [1968:145, 150, 176].

For England and Wales 1861, 1911, and 1931, births by age of mother were obtained from Keyfitz and Flieger [1968:520, 526, 529]. Total births for 1930 were taken from Great Britain, Registrar-General [1932: Text, p. 119]. The ratio (total births 1930)/(total births 1931) was then applied to the Keyfitz and Flieger births by age for 1931 to give estimated 1930 births by age. Births by age of mother for 1950 were obtained from Great Britain, Registrar-General [1952: Tables, Part 2, Civil, p. 140]. Births by age of mother for 1965 were taken from United Nations Demographic Yearbook [1968:254].

For New Zealand births by age of mother for 1912 were obtained from Bunle [1954:305]. Total 1911 births were taken from New Zealand, Government Statistician [1912:303]. Births by age of mother for 1911 were then estimated by applying the ratio (total births 1911)/(total births 1912) to the 1912 births by age. Births by age of mother for 1930, 1950, and 1965 were obtained from New Zealand, Census and Statistics Office [1931a:6] and New Zealand, Dept. of Health [1953:6; 1965:13, 23].

For England and Wales in 1861 deaths from Maternal causes were obtained from Great Britain, House of Commons [1863: vol. 14]. The 1861 statistics in fact pertain just to England and not to England and Wales. Deaths were given in 5-year age groups, except for 25-34 and 35-44. Within each of these age groups deaths were interpolated into 5-year groups by assuming that the age distribution of maternal deaths was the same as that of total deaths.

SOURCES OF AND ADJUSTMENTS TO DATA FOR THE MARITAL STATUS ANALYSIS OF CHAPTER 7

Deaths and population by age and sex for the United States in 1950, France in 1951, and Germany in 1961 were obtained from Keyfitz and Flieger [1968:150,334,352]. All death and population data by marital status and cause were adjusted to be consistent with the Keyfitz and Flieger data in a manner similar to that used in Chapters 3 and 4.

For the United States in 1950 population data by age, sex,

and marital status were obtained from the 1950 Census of Population, Vol. II, Part 1, Detailed Tables, Table 102. For France in 1951, and West Germany in 1961, population data by age, sex, and marital status were obtained from France, INSEE [1955:69] and Germany, Statistisches Bundesamt [1966a]. The French population was given in conventional abridged life table age groups out to age 80. The 80+ age group for each sex-marital group was separated into 80-84 and 85+ using the corresponding proportions in each of these latter age groups in 1954 [France, INSEE, 1968].

United States 1950 deaths by age, sex, cause, and marital status (averaged for 1949-1951) were obtained from US, HEW, PHS [1956a]. France 1951 deaths by age, sex, cause, and marital status (averaged for 1950-1952) were obtained from France, INSEE [1955:69]. Germany 1961 deaths by age, sex, cause, and marital status were obtained from Germany, Statistisches Bundesamt [1966b]. For the United States and France these deaths were not presented in conventional abridged life table age groups. In the United States the age groupings were conventional except for 25-34, 35-44, and 45-54. In France the age groupings were 20-29, 30-39,. . ., 60-69, and 70+. The procedure by which mortality in the unconventional age groups was interpolated into conventional groups assumed that the sex-marital status-cause-specific ratios of death rates between conventional groups were the same as the corresponding sex-cause-specific ratios between the same age groups for all marital statuses combined.

COMPARABILITY OF CAUSE-OF-DEATH DATA OVER TIME AND BETWEEN COUNTRIES

The vital statistics-gathering countries decided around the end of the last century to institute uniform classification of

causes of death. Representatives met in Paris in 1900 and
decided on the first International List of Causes of Death. They
also decided to meet every ten years to revise the list to keep
up with medical progress. These list revisions pose problems
of comparability over time.

The cause categories of Chapters 3 and 4 were designed to
be broad enough that most variations in classification over time
would be contained within them. For example, the detailed
classification of a death from a particular type of respiratory
disease might change over time, but probably it would still be
contained within a broadly defined respiratory category.

The ICD list numbers for the causes used in Chapters 3 and
4 are given in Table A.1. The biggest classification changes
occurred with the Sixth Revision in 1948. Until then most
countries had used the WHO *Manual of Joint Causes of Death*
to decide the underlying cause of death in cases where more
than one condition were present. In 1948 this was changed so
that the examining physician used his own judgment in deciding
the underlying cause.

In the United States 1950 deaths were tabulated first according to the Fifth Revision and then according to the Sixth Revision. Comparability ratios were calculated for both detailed
causes and broad groups of causes [US, HEW, PHS, 1964a].
Large departures from unity were recorded for many of the
detailed causes, but for the causes in Table A.1 almost all the
variations were between .9 and 1.1. Comparability ratios for
the Sixth and Seventh Revisions were much closer to one
[US, HEW, PHS, 1965b]. Since the causes appear reasonably
comparable between the Fifth and Sixth Revisions, where
large classification changes occurred, comparability for earlier
revisions is probably also reasonably good. As discussed in the
text, the most serious problem of comparability encountered
was an apparent shift over time of diagnoses out of the senility
and ill-defined conditions category (part of the "other" category) into the cardiovascular-renal and neoplasms categories.

Table A.1

ICD LIST NUMBERS FOR CAUSES USED IN THE AGE-CAUSE ANALYSIS OF CHAPTERS 3 AND 4

Cause	Revisions			
	2nd (1909)	3rd (1920)	4th (1929)	6th and 7th (1948, 1955)
I-P	1-9, 11-25, 28-35, 37-38, 106-107	1-10, 12-42, 115-116	1-10, 12-44	1-138
C-R	47, 64-65, 77-85, 119-120, 142	51, 74, 83, 87-96, 128-129, 151	56, 82, 90-103, 130-132	330-334, 400-468, 590-594
NEO	39-46, 53, 129, 131	43-50, 65, 137, 139	45-55, 72ab, 139a	140-239
RESP	10, 86-98	11, 97-107	11, 104-114	470-527, 763
DIG	99-105, 108-115, 117-118	108-114, 117-127	115-129	530-587, 764
MAT	134-141	143-150	140-150	640-689
INF	151-153	160-163	158-162	760-762, 765-766
ACC	56-59, 155-186	66-68, 165-203	75-77, 163-198	800-999

A different cause classification was used in the marital status analysis of Chapter 7, shown in Table A.2. Germany used its own list instead of the International List. General arteriosclerosis is included in the "other" category for all three countries. Deaths from this cause were not published by marital status for France and therefore were not included in the cardiovascular-renal category. For the United States deaths from rheumatic fever were not published by marital status, and rheumatic fever was therefore not included in the cardio-vascular-renal category for that country, whereas for France and Germany it is included. Since rheumatic fever accounts for only a tiny proportion of total cardiovascular-renal deaths, this defect in comparability between countries is negligible.

Table A.2

ICD LIST NUMBERS FOR THE CAUSES USED IN THE MARITAL STATUS ANALYSIS OF CHAPTER 7

Cause	US 1950 6th Revision (1948)	France 1951 6th Revision (1948)	Germany 1961 Deutsche Verzeichniss (1958)
TB	1-19	1-19	0-39
SYPH	20-29	20-29	51-59
NEO	140-205, 210-239	140-205, 210-239	201-279
DIAB	260	260	331
C-R	330-334, 410-447, 590-594	330-334, 410-447, 590-594	371-372, 401-472, 701-705
RESP	480-493, 500, 502	480-493, 500-502	521-522, 531, 533, 538, 541, 549
DIG	540, 541, 560, 561, 570, 581	540, 541, 560, 561, 570, 581	611-612, 641, 672
MAT	640-689	Not published; included in Other category	751-779
ACC	800-999	800-999	901-999

Appendix B   Methods of Life Table Construction

The method of life table construction used in all except Chapter 6 of this study represents a minor improvement to Keyfitz's [1968a, 1968b, 1970] iterative life table. For the middle of the table, ages 5 to 80, the strategy is to obtain from each iterate of the life table a set of $_5M'_x$ comparable with the observed $_5M_x$ and to use the ratios $_5M_x/_5M'_x$ to improve the values of $_5q_x$. From the improved values $_5q^*_x$, a new improved life table is calculated, a new set of $_5M'_x$ is worked out, and the procedure repeats until the values $(_5M'_x - _5M_x)$ are as close to zero as desired. Convergence can be speeded by iterating directly on the ℓ_x column, as described by Keyfitz [1970].

In more detail, we begin with the ℓ_5 obtained from calculations for the beginning of the life table and an arbitrary set of values for $\ell_{10}, \ell_{15}, \ldots, \ell_{80}$, to be improved by iteration. We suppose that the population is sectionally stable; i.e., at age x the population density function is of the form

$$k(x) = A\ e^{-rx}\ \ell(x), \tag{B.1}$$

where r is taken to be constant over each overlapping 15-year age interval centered on x+2.5, and A is a constant of proportionality for that age interval. Then

$$_5K'_x = \int_0^5 k(x+u)\ du = A \int_0^5 e^{-r(x+u)}\ \ell(x+u)\ du \tag{B.2}$$

and

$$_5D'_x = A \int_0^5 e^{-r(x+u)} \ell(x+u)\, \mu(x+u)\, du \qquad (B.3)$$

The value of r is calculated from characteristics of the age structure of the observed population and the previous iterate of the life table, and μ is calculated as a function of ℓ and x. The values of $_5M'_x$ are obtained as $_5D'_x$ /$_5K'_x$ and evaluated by integral approximation. For details, the reader is referred to the original papers.

The improvement involves distinguishing the age dimension x from the time dimension t and calculating a slightly more accurate expression for M'_x, which we can denote as M''_x.

We wish to calculate M''_x by taking deaths over the entire year for age group x to x+5 and dividing by the midyear population, reproducing the procedure by which age-specific mortality rates are actually computed. In the Lexis diagram below this means taking a double integral over the entire rectangle to get deaths and taking a line integral over x at time t + 1/2 to get the midyear population. Sectional stability

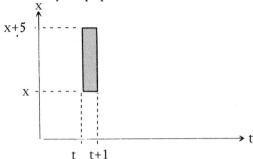

is assumed over the entire rectangle in the x-t plane, thus encompassing the time interval as well as the age interval under consideration. In this rectangle the sectionally stable population is a function of both x and t. We have in place of (B.1) - (B.3)

$$k(x,t) = A\ e^{rt}\ e^{-rx}\ \ell(x) \tag{B.4}$$

$$_5 K''_x = \int_0^5 k(x+u,t+1/2)\ du = A \int_0^5 e^{r(t+1/2)}\ e^{-r(x+u)}\ \ell(x+u)\ du \tag{B.5}$$

$$_5 D''_x = \int_0^1 \int_0^5 k(x+u,t+v)\ \mu(x+u)\ du\ dv$$

$$= A \int_0^1 \int_0^5 e^{r(t+v)}\ e^{-r(x+u)}\ \ell(x+u)\ \mu(x+u)\ du\ dv \tag{B.6}$$

From (B.4) - (B.6) we have, upon simplifying

$$_5 M''_x = \frac{_5 D''_x}{_5 K''_x} = \left(\frac{e^r - 1}{r\ e^{r/2}}\right)\ {_5 M'_x} \tag{B.7}$$

Equation (B.7) is thus identical to Keyfitz's result except for the correction factor $(e^r - 1)/(r\ e^{r/2})$, approximately equal to $(1 + r^2/24)$. For time periods in excess of one year, say m years, it is easy to show that the correction factor is $(e^{rm} - 1)/(rm\ e^{rm/2})$, approximately equal to $(1 + r^2 m^2/24)$. Since the correction factor is greater than 1, we see that Keyfitz's $_5 M'_x$ are understated, the final $_5 q_x$ overstated, and the final ℓ_x understated. For countries with low values of r, however, such as those considered in this study, the improvements are numerically very small. For example, life expectancy at birth is usually unaffected out to tenths of a year.

Chapter 6, on the effects of smoking on the SMD, used Chiang's [1968:203ff] life table method in place of Keyfitz's iterative method. The iterative method is cumbersome to apply when mortality data are available only for a restricted age range, and it will be recalled that data in Chapter 6 were available only for ages 37-86.

Appendix C Discussion of the Residual Terms in the Decompositions

In the text tables using life expectancy as the basic mortality measure, the interpretation of residual terms raises a question: Do these residual terms represent empirical interactions between mortality changes in different age-cause categories? An example of a real empirical interaction would be the increase in mortality from pneumonia during an influenza epidemic. It is immediately clear that the residual terms do not represent empirical interactions, because the variation of mortality in one age-cause category at a time, with mortality in other age-cause categories artificially held constant, constitutes by definition independent variation of mortality in different age-cause categories. (The same point holds true of a slightly modified procedure of varying mortality in one age-cause category at a time, adapted from the multiple decrement literature on competing risks and discussed in Chapter 3. This procedure allows for slight age-distributionally induced perturbations in age-specific mortality rates from one cause when mortality from another cause is independently varied.)

The point that the residuals do not measure empirical interactions is also demonstrated by the previously proved fact that they are uniformly zero when the M-F difference in the age-standardized death rate is used in place of the F-M difference in e_0 (Chapter 3). Since for exactly the same set of initial mortality data the residuals are nonzero in one case and zero in the other, it is clear that they must represent mathematical and not empirical interactions.

The fact that empirical interactions are not reflected in the residual terms does not mean that they are not present. On the contrary, Bayo has pointed out that the elimination (reduction, in the present paper) from a life table of mortality from a specific cause of death, with mortality from other causes held constant, implies that all empirical interactions between the eliminated cause and the remaining causes are preserved. That is, the disease or morbidity corresponding to the eliminated cause is assumed to persist just until the eliminated death, at which point the individual is implicitly assumed to return to a "normal state of health." If the disease or morbidity were removed as well as the corresponding death, the mortality rates from remaining causes would be lowered instead of constant, because the eliminated disease or condition would no longer contribute toward earlier deaths from other causes [US, HEW, 1968:4].

Although the residual terms cannot be interpreted empirically, the possibility remains that they can be interpreted mathematically. However, I have been unable to discover any simple relationships between the residuals and changes in other demographic variables. On the other hand, it can be shown that in a situation of declining mortality and widening sex mortality differentials, the residuals are usually positive.

This is shown first for the decomposition of a change in e_0, and then for the more complicated case of the decomposition of a change in the F-M difference in e_0. If $\mu(x)$ is the force of mortality at age x, $\ell(x)$ the probability of surviving from birth to age x, $\mu_i(x)$ the force of mortality for the ith cause of death, and $\ell_i(x)$ the probability of surviving to age x in the hypothetical case that the ith cause of death is the only cause present, then

$$\ell(x) = \exp\left(-\int_0^x \mu(x)\,dx\right) \qquad\qquad (C.1)$$

$$\ell_i(x) = \exp\left(-\int_0^x \mu_i(x)\,dx\right). \qquad\qquad (C.2)$$

For the simplified case of two causes,

$$\mu(x) = \mu_1(x) + \mu_2(x) \tag{C.3}$$

and, from equations (C.1) to (C.3),

$$\ell(x) = \ell_1(x)\,\ell_2(x). \tag{C.4}$$

For a mortality change between t and t′, we define

$$\Delta\ell_i(x) = \ell_i^{(t')}(x) - \ell_i^{(t)}(x). \tag{C.5}$$

Since

$$e_0 = \int_0^\omega \ell(x)\,dx \tag{C.6}$$

(ω being the maximum age attained), it follows that

$$e_0^{(t')} = \int_0^\omega [\ell_1^{(t)}(x) + \Delta\ell_1(x)]\,[\ell_2^{(t)}(x) + \Delta\ell_2(x)]\,dx. \tag{C.7}$$

Utilizing equations (C.4) to (C.6), we expand and rearrange equation (C.7) to obtain for the change in life expectancy between times t and t′

$$\Delta e_0 = \int_0^\omega \ell_2^{(t)}(x)\,\Delta\ell_1(x)dx + \int_0^\omega \ell_1^{(t)}(x)\,\Delta\ell_2(x)\,dx$$

$$+ \int_0^\omega \Delta\ell_1(x)\,\Delta\ell_2(x)\,dx \tag{C.8}$$

Equation (C.8) gives a cause decomposition of the change in life expectancy over time. The first two terms represent the cause contributions, each obtained by varying mortality from one cause while holding constant mortality from the other cause. The third term is the residual. If mortality is uniformly declining for both causes, so that $\Delta\ell_i(x)$ is positive for all i and x, then both cause and residual contributions are positive. If, instead of two causes, three or more causes are considered in equations (C.7) and (C.8) the residual turns out to be a sum of subcomponent terms, but the above conclusions still hold.

That the cause contributions in (C.8) are equivalent to those obtained by the procedure used in the text of varying mortality in one cause category at a time can be seen more clearly as follows. Let $\ell_{(-i)}(x)$ represent life table survivors with the ith cause deleted. Then the ith cause contribution in (C.8) can be written in general form (valid regardless of the number of causes included in the decomposition) as

$$\int_0^\omega \ell_{(-i)}^{(t)}(x) \; \Delta\ell_i(x) \, dx. \tag{C.9}$$

From equations (C.5) and (C.6), (C.9) becomes

$$\int_0^\omega \ell_{(-i)}^{(t)}(x) \; \ell_i^{(t')}(x) \, dx \; - \int_0^\omega \ell_{(-i)}^{(t)}(x) \; \ell_i^{(t)}(x) \, dx = e_0^* - e_0^{(t)}, \tag{C.10}$$

where e_0^* is the value of life expectancy obtained by letting mortality from the ith cause take on its values at time t' while holding constant mortality from the other causes. The equivalence of the two procedures is thus demonstrated.

If the ith "cause" of death is interpreted abstractly to refer to mortality in either a single age category, a single ICD cause category, or a single age-cause category, the above arguments can be generalized to show that the residual term in any row or column of the complete age-cause decomposition of Δe_0 is positive if all the $\Delta\ell_i(x)$ pertaining to that row or column are positive. It follows that subdivision of a "cause" category results in subcontributions that do not quite add to the original contribution.

For the change in the F-M difference in e_0, the situation is somewhat more complicated. If we consider two equations of the form of (C.8), one for males and one for females, and obtain a third equation of term-by-term differences by subtracting the male equation from the female equation, we obtain a cause decomposition of the change in the F-M difference in e_0. The reader can demonstrate that cause contributions and residuals will all be positive if

$$\Delta \ell_i^f(x) > \Delta \ell_i^m(x) \text{ for all i and x.}$$

In reality, of course, the above inequality is not necessarily in the same direction for all values of i and x pertaining to a given row or column of a decomposition table, and in this case the sign of the corresponding residual cannot be predicted from simple examination of the above questions. In practice, however, the residual in a given row or column usually has the same sign as the corresponding marginal total.

References

Ad Hoc Committee on Dietary Fat and Atherosclerosis. 1961. Dietary Fat and its Relation to Heart Attacks and Strokes. *Circulation* 23:133-136.

Arriaga, E. A., and Davis, K. 1969. The Pattern of Mortality Change in Latin America. *Demography* 6:223-242.

Auerbach, O., *et al.* 1965. Smoking in Relation to Atherosclerosis of the Coronary Arteries. *New England Journal of Medicine* 268:569-574.

Buechley, R. W., *et al.* 1958. Height, Weight, and Mortality in a Population of Longshoremen. *Journal of Chronic Diseases* 7:363-378.

Bunle, H., ed. 1954. *Le Mouvement Naturel de la Population dans le Monde de 1906 à 1936.* Paris: Imprimerie Nationale.

Caffrey, B. 1967. A Review of Empircil Findings. *Milbank Memorial Fund Quarterly* 45 (Pt. 2):119-139.

Chiang, C. L. 1968. *Introduction to Stochastic Processes in Biostatistics.* New York: Wiley.

Ciocco, A. 1940a. On the Mortality in Husbands and Wives. *Human Biology* 12:508-531.

_____. 1940b. Sex Differentials in Morbidity and Mortality. *Quarterly Review of Biology* 15:59-73, 192-210.

Cox, P. R., and Ford, J. R. 1964. The Mortality of Widows, Shortly After Widowhood. *The Lancet* 7325:163-164.

Davis, K. 1965a. Sociological Aspects of Genetic Control. In *Genetics and the Future of Man*, J. D. Roslansky, ed. Amsterdam: North-Holland.

_____. 1965b. The Urbanization of the Human Population. *Scientific American* 213:41-53.

Dorn, H. F. 1961. The Increasing Mortality from Chronic Respiratory Diseases. In *Proceedings of the Social Statistics Section of the American Statistical Association*: 148-152.

_____, and McDowell, A. J. 1939. The Relationship of Fertility and Longevity. *American Sociological Review* 4:234-246.

Dublin, L. I., *et al.* 1949. *Length of Life.* New York: Ronald Press.

El-Badry, M. A. 1969. Higher Female than Male Mortality in Some Countries of South Asia: A Digest. *Journal of the American Statistical Association* 64:1234-1244.

Enterline, P. E. 1960. A Study of Factors Associated with Male-Female Differentials in Mortality. Unpublished Ph.D. dissertation, Department of Sociology, American University, Washington, D.C.

_____. 1961. Causes of Death Responsible for Recent Increases in Sex Mortality Differentials in the United States. *Milbank Memorial Fund Quarterly* 39:312-328.

Fox, S. M., and Skinner, J. S. 1964. Physical Activity and Cardiovascular Health. *American Journal of Cardiology* 14:731-746.

France, Institut National de la Statistique et des Etudes Economiques. 1955. Note sur les Causes de Décès Suivant l'Etat Matrimonial. *Bulletin Mensuel de Statistique,* Nouvelle Série, Supplement, Juillet-Septembre:69.

_____. INSEE. 1968. *Population par Sexe, Age et Etat Matrimonial de 1851 à 1962.* Etudes et Documents Demographiques, No. 10. Paris: Imprimerie Nationale.

Freeman, B. C. 1935. Fertility and Longevity of Married Women Dying after the End of the Reproductive Period. *Human Biology* 7:392-418.

Germany (West). Statistisches Bundesamt. 1966a. *Bevölkerung nach Alter und Familienstand.* Bevölkerung and Kultur, Volks- und Berufszählung vom 6. Juni 1961, Heft 4. Wiesbaden: Statistisches Bundesamt.

_____. SB. 1966b. *Sterbefälle nach Todesursachen, Altersgruppen und Familienstand, 1961.* Bevölkerung and Kultur, Fachserie A, Reihe 7, Gesundheitswesen, Sonderbeitrag. Wiesbaden: Statistisches Bundesamt.

Giersten, J. C. 1965. Atherosclerosis in an Autopsy Series 5: Relation of Coronary Atherosclerosis to Age and Sex. *Acta Pathologica et Microbiologica Scandinavica* 65:245-254.

Gove, W. R. 1973. Sex, Marital Status, and Mortality. *American Journal of Sociology* 79:45-67.

Grannis, G. F. 1970. Demographic Perturbations Secondary to Cigarette Smoking. *Journal of Gerontology* 25:55-63.

Great Britain. House of Commons. 1863. Annual Report of the Registrar-General of Births, Deaths, and Marriages in England 1861. *Sessional*

Papers, Vol. 14.

_____. HC. 1914. Annual Report of the Registrar-General of Births, Deaths, and Marriages in England and Wales 1911. *Sessional Papers,* Vol. 13.

_____. Registrar-General. 1932, 1952, 1967. *Statistical Review of England and Wales* (for 1930, 1950, and 1965). London: H. M. Stationery Office.

Greville, T. N. E. 1948. Mortality Tables Analyzed by Cause of Death. *The Record: American Institute of Actuaries* 37:283-294.

Hamilton, J. B. 1948. The Role of Testicular Secretions as Indicated by the Effects of Castration in Man and by Studies of Pathological Conditions and the Short Lifespan Associated with Maleness. *Recent Progress in Hormone Research* 3:257-324.

Hammond, E. C. 1966. Smoking in Relation to the Death Rates of One Million Men and Women. In *Epidemiological Approaches to the Study of Cancer and Other Chronic Diseases,* W. Haenszel, ed. National Cancer Institute Monograph 19. Washington, D.C.: Government Printing Office.

_____. 1969. Life Expectancy of American Men in Relation to Their Smoking Habits. *Journal of the National Cancer Institute* 43:951-962.

_____, and Horn, D. 1958. Smoking and Death Rates—Report on 44 Months of Follow-Up of 187,783 Men. *Journal of the American Medical Association* 166:1294-1308.

Jacobson, P. H. 1959. *American Marriage and Divorce.* New York: Rinehart.

Jolliffe, N., and Archer, M. 1959. Statistical Associations between International Coronary Heart Diseases Death Rates and Certain Environmental Factors. *Journal of Chronic Diseases* 9:636-652.

Kermack, W. O., *et al.* 1934. Death Rates in Great Britain and Sweden: Some General Regularities and Their Significance. *The Lancet* 226: 698-703.

Keyfitz, N. 1968a. A Life Table That Agrees with the Data: II. *Journal of the American Statistical Association* 63:1253-1268.

_____. 1968b. *Introduction to the Mathematics of Population.* Menlo Park: Addison-Wesley.

_____. 1970. Finding Probabilities from Observed Rates or How to Make a Life Table. *The American Statistician* 24:28-33.

_____, and Flieger, W. 1968. *World Population: An Analysis of Vital*

Data. Chicago: University of Chicago Press.

Keys, A. 1954. Obesity and Degenerative Heart Disease. *American Journal of Public Health* 44:864-871.

Kiser, C. V., *et al.* 1968. *Trends and Variations in Fertility in the United States.* Cambridge: Harvard University Press.

Kitagawa, E. M. 1955. Components of a Difference between Two Rates. *Journal of the American Statistical Association* 50:1168-1194.

_____, and Hauser, P. M. 1973. *Differential Mortality in the United States: A Study in Socioeconomic Epidemiology.* Cambridge: Harvard University Press.

Kraus, A. S., and Lilienfeld, A M. 1959. Some Epidemiological Aspects of the High Mortality Rate in the Young Widowed Group. *Journal of Chronic Diseases* 10:207-217.

Ledermann, S. 1964. *Alcool, Alcoolisme, Alcoolization.* Institut National d'Etudes Démographiques, Travaux et Documents, Cahier No. 41. Paris: Presses Universitaires de France.

Lilienfeld, A. 1959. Emotional and Other Selected Characteristics of Cigarette Smokers and Non-Smokers as Related to Epidemiological Studies of Lung Cancer and Other Diseases. *Journal of the National Cancer Institute* 22:259-282.

Madigan, F. C. 1957. Are Sex Mortality Differentials Biologically Caused? *Milbank Memorial Fund Quarterly* 35:202-223.

Malmros, H. 1950. The Relation of Nutrition to Health. *Acta Medica Scandinavica.* Supplementum 246:137-153.

Marks, H. M. 1960. Influence of Obesity on Morbidity and Mortality. *Bulletin of the New York Academy of Medicine* 36 (Series 2):296-312.

Marks, R. V. 1967. A Review of Empirical Findings. *Milbank Memorial Fund Quarterly* 45 (Part 2):51-107.

Martin, W. J. 1951. A Comparison of the Trends of Male and Female Mortality. *Journal of the Royal Statistical Society* (Jo. A) 144:287-298.

McKeown, T., and Brown, R. G. 1955. Medical Evidence Related to English Population Changes in the Eighteenth Century. *Population Studies* 9:119-141.

Moriyama, I. M. 1948. Statistical Studies of Heart Diseases I: Heart Diseases and Allied Causes of Death in Relation to Age Changes in the Population. *Public Health Reports* 63:537-545.

_____, *et al.* 1958. Observations on Possible Factors Responsible for the Sex and Race Trends in Cardiovascular-Renal Mortality in the

United States. *Journal of Chronic Diseases* 7:401-412.

_____, and Woolsey, T. D. 1951. Statistical Studies of Heart Disease, IX: Race and Sex Differences in Cardiovascular-Renal Mortality from the Major Cardiovascular-Renal Diseases. *Public Health Reports* 66: 355-368.

Morris, J., and Crawford, M. 1958. Coronary Heart Disease and Physical Activity of Work. *British Medical Journal* 2:1485.

Mulcahy, R., *et al.* 1970. Cigarette Smoking Related to Geographic Variations in Coronary Heart Disease Mortality and to Expectation of Life in the Two Sexes. *American Journal of Public Health* 60: 1515-1521.

National Diet-Heart Study. 1968. National Diet-Heart Study Final Report. *Circulation* 37: Supplement No. 1.

New Zealand. 1911, 1916, 1945, 1951, 1965. *Census of Population.* Wellington: Government Printer.

_____. Census and Statistics Office. 1931a. *Report on Vital Statistics of the Dominion of New Zealand for the Year 1930.* Wellington: Government Printer.

_____. C&S. 1931b. *Statistical Report on Population and Buildings for the Year 1930-31.* Wellington: Government Printer.

_____. Department of Health. 1953. *Report on the Medical Statistics of New Zealand for the Year 1950.* Wellington: Government Printer.

_____. DH. 1965. *Medical Statistics Report. Part 1: Mortality and Demographic Data.* Wellington: Government Printer.

_____. Government Statistician. 1912. *Statistics of the Dominion of New Zealand for the Year 1911.* Wellington: Government Printer.

Pearl, R. 1939. The Search for Longevity. *Scientific Monthly* 46:462-483.

Preston, S. H. 1968. Analysis of a Change in Western Mortality Patterns. Unpublished Ph.D. dissertation, Department of Economics, Princeton University.

_____. 1970a. An International Comparison of Excessive Adult Mortality. *Population Studies* 24:5-20.

_____. 1970b. *Older Male Mortality and Cigarette Smoking.* Berkeley: Institute of International Studies, University of California.

_____, Keyfitz, N., and Schoen, R. 1972. *Causes of Death: Life Tables for National Populations.* New York: Seminar Press.

Retherford, R. D. 1970. Analysis of Trends in Sex Mortality Differentials in Developed Countries. Unpublished Ph.D. dissertation, Department of Sociology, University of California, Berkeley.

———. 1972. Tobacco Smoking and the Sex Mortality Differential. *Demography* 9:203-216.

———. 1973. Cigarette Smoking and Widowhood in the United States. *Population Studies* 28:193-206.

Rivin, A. U., and Dimitroff, S. P. 1954. The Incidence and Severity of Atherosclerosis in Estrogen-Treated Males, and in Females with a Hypoestrogenic or a Hyperestrogenic State. *Circulation* 9:533-539.

Shapiro, S., *et al.* 1968. *Infant, Perinatal, Maternal, and Childhood Mortality in the United States.* Cambridge: Harvard University Press.

Sheps, M. 1961. Marriage and Mortality. *American Journal of Public Health* 51:547-555.

Shurtleff, D. 1956. Mortality Among the Married. *Journal of the American Geriatrics Society* 4:654-666.

Smith, T. 1967. A Review of Empirical Findings. *Milbank Memorial Fund Quarterly* 45 (Part 2):23-39.

Spiegelman, M. 1968. Mortality in the United States: A Review and Evaluation of Special Reports of the National Center of Health Statistics. *Demography* 5:525-533.

Stamler, J., *et al.* 1956. Experiences in Assessing Estrogen Antiatherogenesis in the Chick, the Rabbit, and Man. *Annals of the New York Academy of Science* 64 (Art. 4):596-619.

———. 1963. Effectiveness of Estrogens for the Long-Term Therapy of Middle-Aged Men with a History of Myocardial Infarction. In *Coronary Heart Disease: The Seventh Hahnemann Symposium,* W. Likoff and J. H. Moyer, eds. New York: Grune and Stratton.

Stolnitz, G. J. 1956. A Century of International Mortality Trends: II. *Population Studies* 10:17-42.

Strom, A., and Jensen, R. A. 1951. Mortality from Circulatory Diseases in Norway, 1940-1945. *The Lancet* 6647:126-129.

United Nations. 1962. *Population Bulletin of the United Nations No. 6.* New York: United Nations.

———. 1968. *Demographic Yearbook 1967.* New York: United Nations.

United States. Bureau of the Census. 1910, 1930. *Mortality Statistics.* Washington, D.C.: Government Printing Office.

———. BC. 1921. *United States Life Tables 1890, 1901, 1910, and 1901-1910.* Washington, D.C.: Government Printing Office.

———. BC. 1943. *Vital Statistics Rates in the United States, 1900-*

1940 (F. E. Linder and R. D. Grove). Washington, D.C.: Government Printing Office.

———. BC. 1950, 1960a. *Census of Population.* Washington, D.C.: Government Printing Office.

———. BC. 1960b. *Historical Statistics of the United States, Colonial Times to 1957.* Washington, D.C.: Government Printing Office.

———. Department of Agriculture. 1953. *Consumption of Food in the United States, 1900-1952.* Agricultural Handbook No. 62. Washington, D.C.: Government Printing Office.

———. DA. 1960. *Heights and Weights of Adults in the United States.* Home Economics Research Report No. 10. Washington, D.C.: Government Printing Office.

———. Department of Health, Education, and Welfare. Public Health Service. 1950, 1965a. *Vital Statistics of the United States.* Washington, D.C.: Government Printing Office.

———. HEW. PHS. 1956a. Mortality from Selected Causes by Marital Status, United States, 1949-51. *Vital Statistics—Special Reports,* Vol. 39, No. 7.

———. HEW. PHS. 1956b. *Tobacco Smoking Patterns in the United States.* Public Health Service Monograph No. 45. Washington, D.C.: Government Printing Office.

———. HEW. PHS. 1960. Fertility Tables for Birth Cohorts of American Women. *Vital Statistics—Special Reports,* Vol. 51, No. 1.

———. HEW. PHS. 1964a. Comparability Ratios Based on Mortality Statistics for the Fifth and Sixth Revisions: United States 1950. *Vital Statistics—Special Reports,* Vol. 51, No. 3.

———. HEW. PHS. 1964b. *Smoking and Health.* Washington, D.C.: Government Printing Office.

———. HEW. PHS. 1965b. Comparability of Mortality Statistics for the Sixth and Seventh Revisions, United States 1958. *Vital Statistics—Special Reports,* Vol. 51, No. 4.

———. HEW. PHS. 1967. *The Health Consequences of Smoking: A Public Health Service Review.* Washington, D.C.: Government Printing Office.

———. HEW. PHS. 1968. *United States Life Tables by Causes of Death: 1959-61.* Vital Statistics of the United States, Life Tables: 1959-61, Vol. 1, No. 6.

———. HEW. PHS. 1970. *Mortality from Selected Causes by Marital*

Status, United States. Vital and Health Statistics, Series 20, Nos. 8a, 8b. Washington, D.C.: Government Printing Office.

_____ . HEW. PHS. 1971. *Leading Components of Upturn in Mortality for Men: United States—1952-67.* Vital and Health Statistics, Series 20, No. 11. Washington, D.C.: Government Printing Office.

Woolsey, T.D., and Moriyama, I. M. 1948. Statistical Studies of Heart Diseases II: Important Factors in Heart Disease Mortality Trends. *Public Health Reports* 63:1247-1273.

World Health Organization. 1909-1955. *Manual of the International Statistical Classification of Diseases, Injuries, and Causes of Death* (2nd through 7th revisions). Geneva: World Health Organization.

Wuest, J. *et al.* 1953. The Degree of Coronary Atherosclerosis in Bilaterally Oophorectomized Women. *Circulation* 7:801-809.

Young, M., *et al.* 1963. The Mortality of Widowers. *The Lancet* 7305:454-456.

Zalokar, J. B. 1960. Marital Status and Major Causes of Death in Women. *Journal of Chronic Diseases* 11:50-60.

Index

Abortion, 63-64

Accidents: and husband-wife mortality, 87; industrial vs. automobile, 29; male-female differentials, 6, 13, 29, 32, 40; and marital status, 83. *See also* ICD, groupings defined

ACS. *See* American Cancer Society studies

Age-cause contributions to SMD, 26-28

Alcoholism, correlation with smoking, 76

American Cancer Society studies, 14, 71, 74, 80, 104

Animal studies, 9, 12, 20

Archer, M., cholesterol study, 16

Atherosclerosis, in CHD mortality, 15; defined, 15; embolism role, 19; in females, 15, 58; with stress, 21. *See also* Cardiovascular-renal diseases

Athletes. *See* Exercise

Auerbach, O., smoking–CHD study, 15

Autopsy studies, 18-19

Biological factors in SMD, 12-13

Bronchitis. *See* Respiratory diseases

Brown, R. G., hospital-home delivery mortality study, 63

Cancer. *See* Neoplasms

Cardiovascular-renal diseases: as cause of death, 6, 56; contribution to SMD, 29-30, 47, 80-82; in husband-wife mortality, 87; relation to marital status, 83-84. *See also* Atherosclerosis

CHD. *See* Coronary heart disease

Chiang, C. L., competing risk formulae development, 41-42

Cholesterol: dietary sources, 15-16; exercise effects on, 19; fat consumption patterns, 16; and premature CHD, 16; stress effects on, 21

Cigarette smoking. *See* Smoking

Ciocco, A., U.S. death-cause studies, 10-87

Circulatory diseases, *See* Cardiovascular-renal diseases

Competing risks of death, 40

Coronary heart disease, 15-21, 77, 78, 80-82, 102. *See also* Cardiovascular-renal diseases

Cox, P. R., widow study, 88-89

CVL (Cerebrovascular lesions). *See* Cardiovascular-renal diseases